Return to Streets of Eternity

Return to Streets of Eternity

Jan Carew

Edited by
Joy Gleason Carew
and Chris Searle

SMOKE STACK BOOKS

Smokestack Books
1 Lake Terrace, Grewelthorpe, Ripon HG4 3BU
e-mail: info@smokestack-books.co.uk
www.smokestack-books.co.uk

Return to Streets of Eternity
Copyright 2015, the estate of Jan Carew, all rights reserved.
Preface copyright Joy Gleason Carew 2015, all rights reserved.
Introduction copyright Chris Searle 2015, all rights reserved.

Cover image: Jan Carew, 'Sunset'
Author photo: Terry Sampson

ISBN 978-0-9927409-8-6

Smokestack Books is represented
by Inpress Ltd

*'Art and literature are like lightning,
for lightning illuminates and is never timid.'*
Jan Carew

Preface

When Jan Carew passed away at the age of ninety-two in December 2012, he had accomplished many things in his long life. But, there remained one last collection of poetry, one on which he had worked for several years: *Return to Streets of Eternity*. This collection recaptures the title of his earliest collection, *Streets of Eternity*, which was published in British Guiana (now Guyana) in 1952, when he was thirty-two and his intellectual, political and artistic life was beginning to gain speed. In compiling this new collection, he has provided 'bookends' to a life well-lived and which would span another six decades and stretch over four continents.

This collection brings together work from his young adulthood in British Guiana; reactions to life's experiences coming out of World War II and his post-War education in the US and Europe; perspectives of the anti-colonial struggle in Europe and at home; and reflections on the very human quest of peoples of colour to shape their own destiny. Jan Carew may have lived most of his life outside of his home country of Guyana, but, as he continuously reminded his readers, the prism, through which he viewed the larger world, was invariably shaped by the village and the communities of his youth.

Known primarily as an author of novels, histories, essay collections, journalism, plays, and as an academic, Jan Carew was, at heart, a poet. He was constantly writing poems or revising earlier ones. Besides this collection, his work has appeared in previous collections of his, *Streets of Eternity* and *Sea Drums in My Blood,* in other collections, as well as in various publications around the world and in many different languages.

Many of these poems refer to key persons or events, thus a 'Notes' section appears at the end of this collection to remind the readers of whom these persons or events are.

Joy Gleason Carew

Introduction

Reading through *Return to Streets of Eternity* is like re-living the greater part of a century of struggle and for betterment in many crucial places in the world, and the moments which seized their people's dreams and strivings. These are poems of hope and optimism, of the movement forever forward, a part of 'the long march from breast to death' along those streets,

> *and resurrection*
> *must renew itself*
> *with every new day*
> *on a calendar of victory.*

So within them are protagonists and heroes like Tiho the Carib, the Ghanaian slave descendants and confederates of Kwame Nkrumah, Cubans, Angolans and Jamaicans, Fedon and Bishop of Grenada, Toussaint L'Ouverture of Haiti, like the child-martyrs of Soweto, Patrice Lumumba of the Congo, Allende of Chile, Cheddi Jagan and Walter Rodney of Guyana, Claudia Jones of Trinidad, New York and London, Mumia Abu-Jamal of the U.S.A. They are all celebrated as essential to the poet's life and utterance, his imagination and experience, and many of them are his contemporaries, living inspirations and exemplars.

Thus *Return to Streets of Eternity* is poetry as a chronicle and history of the poet's life-imagination, made, word by word, from real events transformed by images for all time, so that, as Carew writes in his 'Requiem for Cheddi Jagan':

> *the torment of the poor and despised*
> *must be redeemed forever.*

These 'poor and despised' are the people who are the earth of this poetry: their hopes, lives and struggles. And its words, drenched with aspiration and direction, anticipate the dawn when their freedom will be realised, when

> *the night of vampires must give way to day-clean,*
> *warriors will return to long cool evenings*
> *and the wine jars and the children*
> *chanting poem-hymns and dancing*

Carew writes many poems to his comrades of poetry, for they open up the people's struggles to themselves and to the world beyond. Robin Dobru of Surinam, Dennis Brutus of South Africa, Agostinho Neto of Angola, Andrew Salkey of Jamaica: they are all here, all eternalised too in these avenues of words. And walking in front is another Guyanese bard, the nonpareil of Caribbean poetry, Martin Carter. There are several moments in *Return to Streets of Eternity* when Carew's words could be those of Carter, so essentially Guyanese are they. 'We do not sleep to dream, but dream to change the world', wrote Carter in 'Looking at Your Hands'. In his poem to Rodney called 'The History Maker', Carew tells us that

> *it's only a dream*
> *but when you dream with millions*
> *the dream's like a flower awakening*
> *to trumpet new dawns of reality.*

And remembering the March 1960 massacre of 69 protesting South Africans at Sharpeville in his poem 'I Fight for What Must Be', Carew writes two lines of a raw and naked imaginative beauty and power that are Carter to the core:

> *I fight for what must be and memories that*
> *cling like bark to a tree.*

All these humans: visionaries, activists, militants, martyrs and writers are the living flesh of Carew's poetry and those who walk, proudly and in freedom, along his eternal thoroughfares, so that we can always seek their counsel, talk to them, walk alongside them and join in their courage, clarity, beauty and solidarity. They are, as Carew describes them, 'the heirs of everlasting hope' and they carry our dreams in order to give them back to us:

*The dream that all peoples have a right to share
The water of the River of Life
And drink with their own cups.*

Carew's cups are for us all, and they carry the essence of continuing life, its struggles, its pleasures and its victories.

*Chris Searle
Sheffield, May 2014*

Contents

Rompiendo el silencio
Why Have I Walled in My Poet's Voice?	17
What is My Name?	18
Tiho the Carib	19
The Nomad	20
Sea Drums	21
Africa – America	22
Mahaica	23
Aiomon Kondi	24
Tapawatara	25
Guyanese Three	26
Black and White	27

Our Caribbean
Jamaica – Angola	31
Florida – Angola	33
Florida – Angola II	35
Harlem – Angola	36
The Sea	37
Mad Martha	38
Nocturne for Roots	40
Ikurua	41

Columbus Discovered
Caonabo	45
The Cliffs at Manzanilla	46
Red Indians Never Die	47
Africa – Guyana	48

The Struggle
Catechism of Hope	53
A Chrysalis of Rainbows	55
Toussaint L'Ouverture	59
The Ebony Moors	61
Obote Must Return	63
Who Pays the Piper?	65
Faces and Skulls	66
Housewives in Dearborne	67
The White Sun Dying	68
Ashes and Silence	69
Ballad for a Revolution	71
Building the Great Wall	72

Vulcan Speaks	73
Grenada! Grenada!	74
I Fight for What Must Be	76
If He's Killed We'll Bleed	77
Letter to Agostinho Neto	79
The Children are Dying Quietly	81
The Death of Lumumba	82

Tributes and Requiems

Tribute to Dobru	87
For Buzz	88
Lost Steps I Found	89
Tribute to Claudia	91
Tribute to My Mother	92
Poem for a Boy of Nine Who Left Us	94
For Syl	97
Requiem for Ted Watkins	98
Requiem for Andrew	100
Requiem for My Sister	102
Requiem for Cheddi Jagan	108
On Visiting Phillip Agee	110
Requiem for My Auntie	111
Requiem for the Innocent	112
Requiem for Warren	114
Requiem for Vernon	115
For Martin Carter	117

The Guyanese Wanderer

Before Majorca	121
Prague Revisited	122
Berlin	123
Exile (Toronto)	124
Return to Chicago	126
An Autobiography of Wandering	127
Geneva	130

Cuba

Ten Years: 1959-1969	133
Cuba – Angola	138
The High Road to Harar	140
Our Home	144

Poems of Resistance and Liberation

For Wilson Harris	147
The Children	148
Allende's Daughter	149

Yvette	150
Dobru Speaks to the Children	151
Assassins of Dreams	153

Canadian Poems

Snowtime	157
The Cyclopean Eye	158
The Exile	159
Morning at Lake Simcoe	162
The Hemlock Fringe Before the Pines	164
Morning Writes a Calligraphy With Shadows	165

Star Poems

Canis Major	169
Canis Minor	170
Canopus One	171
Canopus Two	172

Nostalgia

Dreamtime	175
Manaharva's Dream	176
South, to the Land	177
Daydreaming	178
Joanna	179
The Survivor	180

Love Poems

Eternity	183
Chantoba	184
Chantoba II	185
April Twentieth	186
For Joy	187
To Joy	188
Cicada Song	189

Africa

Ballad for Soweto	193
Gems and Dust	194
For Dennis Brutus	196
The History-Maker	198
For Irving Davis	203
Dahomey Dreams	205

Epitaph

A Quiet Passing	209

**Rompiendo
el Silencio**

Why Have I Walled in My Poet's Voice?

Why have I walled in my poet's voice
with cinder blocks of silence
for so long,
when there are still
so many songs of liberation to be sung?
I must go wandering again
Across green pastures of my mind.
I must hurl words
across drawbridges
of wild imaginings
I must re-enter
casements of my soul
and unvault
secrets that were stored there
since I inherited
the breath of life

Louisville, 17 May 2008

What is My Name?

What is my name?
I ask in the resonant silence
The lost centuries shout
you don't know the secret yet
the one that Black Africa has kept?
Why don't you ask
your Ancestor
the Slave
She knows your name
and you'd better listen
She's whispered in your ear
four hundred years
Oh can't you hear
Oh can't you hear
Eduful, Jaja
Yawa, Oto, Loki, Bankole
Take back the name
you've been too deaf to hear
Silence of centuries
has numbed your ears
The black solitudes
must reappear
The answer is near
as sweet as music
to the listening ear

Tiho the Carib

The first time I saw the sea
I did not know
it was not green like parrots
or rainbowed like macaws.
The first time the sea spoke to me
it sounded different
to trees and rivers,
my mother's singing, or
wind combing the hair
of tall savannah grass.
The first time I touched the sea
it licked my feet
with a rough tongue
like a ocelot's,
and wind sang to me:
'Wide the world wide, boy,
wide and deep!
wide the world wide, boy,
wider than the heart can reach,
wide the world wide, boy!'

The Nomad

for A.J. Seymour

The crows that speck my tropic skies
soar over valleys of my green days
where clouds like dice tumble
in windy vortices that tunnel skies.
While I crossed wide Atlantic seas
where seagulls arching to the long sea swells
startled to bells
that rang farewell to Cancer.

But herons still fly to Ichillibar
at day-clean,
and Potaro spins whirlpools
to entomb a boatman's dream.

Sea Drums

I heard sea drums
at El Mina
on the Ghana coast
and echoes boomed
around the curving shores
the very echoes
that Columbus heard
when he palavered
with a midnight king
bargaining for a trading post.
The midnight monarch
towering above
his doubleted petitioners
laughed louder
than the surf
and opened wide
the welcoming gates.
'Come in!' he invited,
and a motley band
trailed warily behind the midnight king,
carrying beads,
and guns,
and powder horns
and murderous Toledo blades;
the Black king and his counselors
soon discovered
that these men from 'heaven'
were suffering from a disease
that only gold could cure.

Evanston, 14 October 1978

Africa – America

for Kwame Nkrumah

Africa – America
two loins astride Atlantic tides
heaving
to answer rhythms
of the sun's hot thrust
conceived and harboured me
in amniotic ease
until a caesarean knife
of slavery
left me naked
outside a cathedral
of Amazonian trees
I greeted my first morning
bawling for life.
Africa – America
two bosoms
guided my lips to nipples
where I fed
and sea-drums echoed
in my blood again.
Africa – America
The breath of life
in music
and fathomless deep oceans
of sorrow.

Evanston, November 1978

Mahaica

Running on flat golden sands
of Mahaica beach
between the sea wall
and an amber sea
Miguel talked about English cadences;
wind and flashing wavelets ignored him.
I, remembering Cassius in Julius Caesar, declaimed:
'I cannot tell what you and other men
think of this life, but for my single self
I would as lief not live to be in awe
of such a thing as I myself . . .'
My voice was hollow,
like wind in a conch shell.
An equatorial breeze
rising like daydreams
swept crows and herons,
wild geese and seagulls
towards the incandescent heart of the sun.
Crabs glittered in burnished mud,
lepers in a nearby asylum
walked like Hamlet's ghost
behind battlements of green hedges.
We ran and ran
until we came
to the River of Singing Birds.

Aiomon Kondi

Aiomon Kondi, dweller in the heights,
saw with his condor eye
a blue buck-crab sky;
white sun lying on black rivers
like a lover;
white sun arched and indolent like an ocelot;
white sun biting the backs of reapers
like a Llanero's whip;
white sun with a heart of darkness
like a sunflower;
white sun falling,
like a wounded crane,
burning itself out
like a comet
or a candle in a cave.

Tapawatara

Drowned flowers
under the running tides
alive
peering out of amber depths
with purple eyes
defying cataracts
adamantine rocks
at Tapawatara
Marrying the singing tides
blind rocks
the cruel sun
indifferent starlight
Siren flowers dancing
to rhythms of water and wind
litanies of death
in the moonlight
I hear you
and I'm tempted to answer
Yes.

Guyanese Three

in remembrance of three of my Guyanese comrades who died in WWII

My home's an old Berbician town
where never ending rains pour down
and myriad birds in ordered flight
wing slowly through swift fading light.

What do I know of Saxon snow
and nights alight with sunlit glow?
I should have died in forests green
where rivers lisp and parrots scream.

My home's a verdant, narrow strand
where long savannahs, wide, unplanned
embrace the blue encircling sky
and eagles touch the fierce sun's eye.

What do I know of raging seas
and pagan rhapsodies of breeze?
I should have died upon a reef
where blossoms crown each dying leaf.

My home's beside a waterfall
where everlasting voices call
and from the gorge you watch all day
at rainbows dancing in the spray.

My body is restless so far from home
I died beyond St. Peter's dome
and poppies in these eyeless fields
are drops of blood my sad heart bleeds.

Black and White

Dreams die
when you are dead
unless you write them
on white leaves
that speak to the ear.

Our Caribbean

Jamaica – Angola

Green sanctuary of hills folded like
fists at Acompong;
granite knuckles threatening,
mahoe trees capturing dew and starlight
through the long nights, and scattering them
when morning winds and spears of sunlight
rend heavy mists to shreds, until they
trail like torn scarves from burning mountain peaks
Palenques of Acompong your dreams of
returning to Africa and home
have been realized
Cuban sons of mothers and maternal aunts
have recrossed the Middle Passage
in Caravelles of Freedom
Palenques of Acompong, do you remember,
do you remember the time of your exile
to winter snows of Nova Scotia;
your imprisonment in seasons
of winter twilight, sunlight invading
the night; unmelodious north winds moaning
in the pines; eyes of Arctic ice
welcoming you?
Palenques of Acompong, your dreams
are realized, poem-hymns to freedom
are caroling in the Sierra Maestra
and echoing across the Lobito plains.
Cuba made the first unequivocal
choices for us all:
the have-nots not the have-gots,
not Caliban enslaved
but Caliban seizing his immemorial heritage
of liberty and death.
Our Caribbean for the first time
became an archipelago of steppingstones
on the road back to Africa and home.

Cuban brothers led the return
With guns in their hands, fury in their hearts,
reverence for the poor,
love for two motherlands – Cuba – Angola!
Of the numberless ones
who had come on a forced journey
of no return, they were the vanguard
the first ones going back to wrest
the ancestral homeland from usurpers.

Florida – Angola

Do you remember? Do you remember?
The invincible ones,
escaped slaves and Seminole runaways
cheating slave catchers
for a hundred years,
making Spanish Florida a sanctuary
for the brave, a landscape of graves
for the buccaneers of profit
High Priests of racial hate.
Noble Osceola, trapped by tricksters
rising from his deathbed to adorn himself
with a cacique's headdress of eagle feathers,
an embroidered tunic of deerskin,
moccasins molded on a last of wind and fire
a shaft of sunlight for his spear.
Do you remember? Do you remember?
How he stood up straight and heard
the laughter of children
and shamans mumbling orisons
to the Mother of Corn, the Wendigo
with burning feet
How listening to the cunning footsteps of Mantop
Death's messenger stalking him
He held a musket high above his head
And cried: 'This is our freedom!'
Echoes clamored across bayous,
fields of wild rice sighed in the listening wind;
cottontails rippled mirror-still waters
and disappeared.
Osceola's war-cry secreted away
in the Heart of Heaven
hid like a hurricane in the cool flesh
of the sea winds.
Atlassa's mother, rocking him
in a cradle of reeds, perfumed

with sassafras and lemon grass
crooned Osceola's war-cry
like a lullaby to him.
Kofi Abraham's mother
hearing its echoings felt her heart kindle
into rebellion. She walked the freedom trail
from Georgia's red earth
to Florida's watery wilderness
'The fruit of my womb must be born free
or I'll die walking these pathless ways
to liberty!'
She sang her African nomad's songs until
Seminoles and Muskogens welcomed her.
Her boychild was born under the bluest sky,
Raindrops and magnolia petals christened him.
Atlassa and Kofi Abraham picked up
The Fallen standards
That fell from Osceola's trembling hands,
Holding them high in the windless swamps
with storms in their hearts
Made reeds and saplings bend in half.
The blood knot held; and no hemorrhage
Of treachery ever divided them.

Florida – Angola II

Africa – Florida
Atlassa and Kofi Abraham slept
In exile graves
The cannonading of victories
From Moncada to the Cubango plains
Awakened them.

Harlem – Angola

Trapped in baracoons of neon lights
palisades of skyscrapers,
blues, jazz, rock, soul, folksongs
ballads as cool as mountain pools
throb out of a placenta of pain.
Witch doctors of rhythm
weighed down with unconscious memories
emerge to cast a spell over the world
Drums and flutes on the Lobito plains
sent rhythms pounding in heartbeats
of ebony cargoes; in minds tormented
by immemorial longings for a lost home
dream-spinners sang the blues,
pacing pavements of destruction.
The night is long but day-clean will come.
Cocks of dawn will be accompanied
by a tenor sax, a bongo, a guitar
and a base beat solid as surf pounding rocks
to the lyrics of freedom songs;
Harlem – Angola!
Angola – Cuba!

The Sea

The sea
turns all men white
Black power drowned
at Castle Bruce
turns up the green rocks at Grand Bay
bleached white as lilies
Those who dream
eternally of being white,
washed with hyssop,
can drown at Castle Bruce
The sea
will make them
whiter than snow
on green rocks
at Grand Bay
wearing blue shrimps for eyes

Mad Martha

Mad Martha sat at the intersection
of Mimosa
and Coburg Street
under a spreading saman tree,
her limbs
filarial
were swollen like cassava roots.
I left Mad Martha
to explore
the wide indifference
of trans-Atlantic dreams.
When I returned
a scholar-man,
emancipated,
Mad Martha was still there
her sightless eyes glittering,
she sensed my presence
and enquired,
'What you bring back, bryga-man?
Can you ease the swelling
in my legs,
or make a yam grow better
than before you left?'
Three grandsons
sped by
in dream-chariots
made in Detroit, Oxford,
Frankfurt-on-Main,
One was a Minister of Sport,
the other
a Permanent Secretary
in the Ministry
of Health
and the third,
a Priest.

Georgetown cynics,
famous for their wit
composed a calypso with a chorus of
'three blind mice see how they run'
'What you just saw flashing past,' she said,
'is my three mistakes
with hit-and-run night riders.'
Mad Martha coughed
and spat
in the dust that rose
in the wake
of their dream chariots.
I was home again.

Nocturne for Roots

My mother left me rocking in a cradle
under tall amarata trees
My mother went to the fields searching for roots
I lay in spangled bowers
where leaves and shadows
clapped hands in the wind
Afternoon sunlight
was the only intruder
Morpho butterflies and red herons
hung like lanterns
on branches above me.
My mother returned
and enlivened the afternoon
with laughter and singing.
Legba, Master of the Crossroads
had led her to green and golden fields
where she found roots
fragrant with earth-smells –
cassava, yams, tanyas, wild eddoes
that turn a seaweed purple
with boiling
My mother carried me on her back
my ear was pressed close
to the drums of her heartbeat
She sang forgotten lullabies
accompanied by a fugue of rainfrogs
and nocturnes of six o'clock bees
Her breath was soft as the hum
of a hummingbird's wings
She hurried home
When darkness blotted out the sunset
At day-clean
the search for roots began again.

Ikurua

The reapers bleed the weeping trees
criss-cross the barks with undeciphered rhymes
and garner tears to nourish their own life.
Who know no sky save panoply of leaves
forget the measured spans of sun
while sickle moon escorted by lone star
blooms inset dew on blades of grass and trees
through the full moon.
Calendar of days is sweat
Dripped jewels from clepsydra of bursting hearts.
Reapers climb the weeping trees,
part canopy of leaves to reach green pinnacles,
expose the sky, bleached parchment of the rolling clouds
write colour, splendour, darkness, light
shadowed and dyed in surfs of whirling universe.
Reapers sing release, lonely like a russet tree
In changing galaxies of green pavements
That line streets of eternity.
Seas of savannahs, carpeted with reeds
Drown frantic roots that claw the earth for life.
Immunity from strife is mirror-pool that
captures heaven in reflected light
and worshippers weave spools of drowned divinities
til the demonic dreamer time
shatters the mirror of still pool, bends halters of the sun and moon
that unity might wear chaotic face.
The weeping trees abandoned to preening time
weep slow and viscous tears
and heedless columns of companion trees
bear witness to undeciphered rhymes.

**Columbus
Discovered**

Caonabo

'Caonabo, Caonabo,'
our first Freedom Fighter,
are tides of Sargasso
still plucking your bones
with a murmur of panpipes?
Does Ojeda's betrayal
still stick
in your throat
like a bone?
Wake up ancestor, Caonabo,
you can go home
to Marien again.

The Cliffs at Manzanilla

for Roberto Retamar

I swear I'll not forget
dawn's dreams that you had spawned
in a green time
Tawny breakers leaping high
like agile tongues to lick the salted spume
and wild palms spinning like green wheels
in the wind
Green rocks and amaryllic shale
were altars where you died
at Manzanilla
Your prayers to Savacou and Hurricane
Immortal gods of Spirit and of Flesh
were lost like echoes of the thrashing surf
in the green indifferent hinterlands of silence
A cannonade of Lombards overcame the magic
of the Lightning-Eel, the Thunder-Axe
and wreaths of foam were strewn
across the amber sand
To be or not to be a slave
left you no choice save suicide
My Carib ancestors I swear
I'll not forget
the green years of your saga
in an ocean sea
that bears your name
eternally.

Red Indians Never Die

Sons of the Shaking Earth
and daughters of the Flying Wind
never die,
they sign a treaty
and fade away.
Mantop, Death's Messenger
with a parchment face,
proffers a quill:
'Sign here,
on the dotted line!'
The dotted line's a code
like broken teeth or tilting gravestones
White leaves that speak to the listening ear,
Whisper a cautionary note
Of past betrayals:
'Brother, you're signing away skies
of Aiomon Kondi, Dweller in the Heights,
Continents and Islands
of Pia and Makunaima, Children of the Sun,
Seascapes of the Lightning-Eel,
the Thunder-Axe,
Firmaments of Hurricanes,
the Heart of Heaven,
the Breath of Life . . .'
'Sign on the dotted line!'
The voice, insists,
and new voices are added in a
firmament of pain.
Sons of the Shaking Earth
and Daughters of the Flying Wind
never die.

Africa – Guyana

Labadi on the Ghana coast
where palm-wine drinkaards listening to surf
roaring in their blood;
lean on moonbeams
the beaches reel
before lips of rising tide edged with spume;
roots are white fangs
bared at the eroding wind and sea;
fishermen in long canoes
part the surf,
and comb the manes of white horses with tridents;
the stench of mud and crabs in the oleous breeze
is a dubious perfume,
dancers sway like kites
and Ewe talking drums converse
Across distances of land and sea.
High tide erases my footprints
from Labadi to the Angola coast
and north to El Jadida.
The middle-Passage,
the reaches of Sargasso,
Atlantis of the legend,
are tombs to house ancestral bones.
Memories of two motherlands—
Africa – Guyana –
scrawled carelessly with broken spears,
and shattered gourds from which I once drank
buried their tribal secrets in the sand
before my parting.
Africa – Guyana!
Drunk as Boshongo Lords,
palm-wine drinkaards chant,
'It was the same mangrove,
the same beaches wreaths of amber foam,
the same sky, dyed a Berber-blue,

the same white clouds passing before the sun
like processions of marabouts.'
What language shall I speak to the lisping tides?
White worshippers of Kali
have long since tightened silken scarves
around ancestral throats.
Labadi is a name to conjure with.
Palm-wine drinkaards sit in magic circles
incanting.
I hear the murmur of my beginnings,
talk to night winds, and tides,
fishermen,
dancing out of a bellows of sea and sky,
hear me speak.
'ABRUNI-MAN! And yet he has my cousin's face,'
they reply.
Our gourds are brimming over.
'I am your cousin's face three centuries away!'
'Where do you hail from again, my brother?'
palm-wine drinkaards chorus drunkenly.
GUYANA! AFRICA – GUYANA, THREE CENTURIES AWAY!
Surf, lisping tides,
palm-wine drinkaards,
and moonlight casting hard, communal shadows
on white sand
listen indifferently.

The Struggle

Catechism of Hope

If you stumble and fall down
before our struggle's won
don't pine any longer
than it takes
for tears to tie themselves
like shoelaces under your chin;
and don't believe for a moment
that flowers won't bloom again
or kiskadees won't sing,
that rivers of the morning
won't sparkle
under the lash of winds,
that mists won't be trapped
like the breath of dreamtime seekers
in fastnesses of dark green hills,
that the Road to Hope
won't glitter for an instant
and then crumble
like the skin
a snake leaves behind him,
that mimosas won't deny their perfume
to long cool evenings.
If you stumble and fall down
before our struggle's won,
stand up!
Wash and bandage your wounds,
spit blood and sing
through a swollen mouth,
sing a wild song
and let it echo
in vortices of your head
like a bellbird's fife, panpipe or flageolet
or like a talking drum.
'Stand up!' I said
and if the noonday sun bandages your eyes,

rip away the bandage, and
cross countless seasons of pain
between day-clean and can't-see-time,
feeling good,
singing a refrain
of the born-again fighters,
and when the night staggers in
like a drunken priest
blotting out the sun
rinse your brain again and again
under a shower of stars.
Don't be afraid of catching cold,
the watchman of day-clean
will turn off the spigot in time
and you'll be ready, primed
to face ten thousand mornings
of a New Day.

Evanston, 8 October 1978

A Chrysalis of Rainbows

Nicaragua – Grenada
A Carnival of Devils
is road-marching itself into oblivion
starlight is denying its illumination
to prima donnas
in a masquerade of death
ghoulish harlequins are shadows
in the light of fireflies and lanterns
puppet-masters of the *dance macabre*
are shambling away
to Mephistophelian lairs.
Nicaragua – Grenada
carnivals of Liberty
are converging
on the Place de la Revolucion
and the Carenage,
Liberty Bells
are ringing across our Caribbean,
oscillating between Pacific and Atlantic tides
memories of Legba, squatting at the intersection
of Streets of Eternity,
Damballa, inscrutable as a starless sky,
Nyankapon and Aiomon Kondi
linking arms in doomed pantheons,
memories fresh and warm
as the milk of mothers
overflowing from the breasts of drums.
The Carnival of Liberty is converging
on the Place de la Revolucion
and the Carenage,
and an eternity of suffering
is banished in a day of victory,
the Dance has ended,
the musicians are shaking the spittle
from their silent flutes

steel bands have struck up
the opening notes of the Road March
and orchestras of flutes, panpipes, guitars, maracas
have taken their cues
the dancers, brilliant as toucans,
are beside themselves with joy
but the precision and power of the rhythms
compel limbs to move in unison
seducing all to sing choruses
with a single voice
the calendar on which time and seasons
had etched ancestral rhythms of life
is marked with sightings of new stars
fresh constellations of liberty.
Nicaragua – Grenada
your revolutions erupted
from the same dark flesh
of our Caribbean earth
that Cuban brothers had first ploughed.
Carnivals of Liberty are converging
on the Place de la Revolucion
and the Carenage,
drums and mandolins, flutes and guitars,
cymbals and lyres, maracas and charangos
steel bands and Mariachis, panpipes and Mayan harps
are building tunes
on a foundation of base beats
as solid as surf
and dancers are strumming responses
with feet as light as the wind.
The erstwhile, mute and invisible ones
have burst upon the centre stage of history
and converged on the Place de la Revolucion
and the Carenage.
Ancestor Fedon has abandoned
his tortoise galleries of the deeps off Grenada
and Brother Sandino has walked away
from a shallow grave

festooned with fallen flowers from towering canopies
and then they sit upon the ground
and swap stories of Viceroys, Generals, Governors of the Night,
tyrants, surrogate proconsuls,
high priests of pure money;
of whips and chains and cages
where dream-spinners were murdered
after they fashioned dazzling threads
to weave the cloth of life;
of husks, and hills bleached to the bone;
of broken ears of corn
flavoured with the droppings of rats;
of slaves and peasant millions,
and numberless mute ones
mired in grief
but rising up to strike and strike again
like pale lightnings in evenings before a New Day.
Brother Sandino and Ancestor Fedon
laugh and weep and embrace
and arm in arm join the carnival crowd
sons of the shaking earth
and sisters of the flying wind
make way for them
and when they reach the podiums
at the Place de la Revolucion and the Carenage
they do a Sun Dance
and a Rain Dance
and a dance to the Mother of Corn
and as their hips gyrate
and their feet move
as light as the wind
a host of fallen martyrs join them,
Ancestor Fedon and Brother Sandino
dance side by side with freedom fighters
whose wounds still gape
like freshly painted lips,
with Indian caciques
and Africans with plumed heads,

Mestizos with torn shirts
Peasants with glittering, obsidian eyes,
city workers with sweat
jewelling their brows;
dance and sing and swirl.
The souls of those who died
to make the world a better place
are entering the gentle hearts
of Quetzl birds.
The long march from breast to death
and resurrection
must renew itself
with every new day
on a calendar of victory.

Kingston, 2 August 1979

Toussaint L'Ouverture

a reverie

Who is a slave and who is free
when anarchy reigns?
I have been vanquished
by my haste to change the world:
Christophe! Dessalines!
pourquoi m'avez-vous trahi?
These sentinel peaks of Jura
are daggers dipped in venom;
the cold demented wind,
moaning in the pine trees,
sneaks underneath my window,
whispering of death and graves
and the putrid delight of maggots.
This fortress of Joux
where I am caged
is sucking my life
into its damp walls:
'Guard! Guard!
give me paper, ink and a quill'
I brought the sun in my blood,
but now
I must move closer to the fire,
and bathe my limbs in flames
'Guard! Guard!'
I have been ordered to give you
nothing on which you can write.
Why do you write, and write?
The Emperor will never reply.
And yet he asks about you
all the time
as though he were afraid.
'Afraid? After pushing me
to the lip of the grave?
Then he's afraid of ghosts
and phantoms

from the forest of everlasting night.'
I am already dead,
but he's afraid of liberty.
The word's a burning ember
on his tongue.
I was born a slave
and now, liberty's the breath of life to me.
I first discovered ancestral legacies
dancing around campfires at night,
and, as I danced,
shadows from the agile flames
striped my body like a tiger's,
and my feet inherited the wind.
Phantom footsteps echo
in the circle of my vacant days
as though ghosts of the fallen
were once more on parade.
I must give the sentries
orders for the night, General L'Ouverture.
'Tell them that
the password:
should be Fear!
Say that I am being buried alive in order
to allay an Emperor's fear.'
Outside, ravens scrawled
shadowed arabesques
on pages of the wind.
When morning came sunlight fell upon a corpse.
The jailer touched the icy face
And sent his final report
To the Emperor:
'General L'Ouverture died last night . . .'
the news winged its way across continents
and an ocean
Toussaint is dead,
but liberty is alive!
The Haitian hills
will trap the morning light again
and the people will sing.

The Ebony Moors

They were a people born at five past midnight,
who, vaulting over seas
between Pillars of Hercules,
brought light to a dark continent
where blood, plague and furies nested
side by side
with twilight thralldoms of hooded minds
left in the wake
of barbarian Vandals and Visigoths
wild Horsemen of Apocalypse.
'Light, more light!'
Goethe had cried long after
from fading landscapes
of his death-dimmed eyes
But Goethe slipped into a Stygian oblivion
Not knowing that Moors were light-bringers;
That Almoravids blood-knotted to Sanhaja kith and kin
with silken African complexions
had come scattering
incandescent sun-flares of enlightenment;
with sheet lightning flashing
from their ivory teeth and ivory eyes;
that breast-fed from the bosom of siroccos
Almoravid women from Sahara's southern rim,
had mothered and bequeathed soul-fires
to soldiers, singers, seers, scholars.
Anthracite sons and daughters of the sun,
culture–bringers jewelling
new cosmoses of the mind
with poem-hymns to Allah
and songs to calyxes of flowers
opening to wind and sun,
ebony poets troubadouring
to shining cities of al-Andalus,
riding winged Arab steeds

across the Pyrenees,
until Martel, the hammer-man
eviscerated their dreams.
Weep for the ebony Moors
whose songs of Africa and home
echo in lamentos of Andalusian gypsies!
Weep for the peerless Almoravid learning
calcined
in inquisitorial fires!

Obote Must Return

I must return to Entebbe again
to the lake of a million flamingoes
Where vultures advertise their trade with blood-red crests
the lake spreads out a golden tablecloth
Wrinkled by wind at sunrise,
the hungry Nile eats before it sets out for the wine-dark sea
And reeds sing.
I stand in elephant grass tall as the listening trees
and sway to the song of snakes and the hiss of reeds
The muted lisping of the Nile
the hum of lakeflies
and songless drums in hollows of my heart
sing ancient requiems of the Langis
The dirge of death before the warriors arise:
'One has fallen but he will arise again
swift as the running tide where leaping hoofs of water
pound the stubborn rocks, laughing to hide their rage
there are tongues under the tides stammering
and who will hear must press ears to the ground
and listen to the message germinate.
The pounding hoofs are muffled in the swamps
leeches fatten on dark blood and cool winds intoxicate
Their vampire dreams sleep at the roots of reeds
in murky caverns where life began.
I part the reeds and hurry to the road
I must go to Kampala and the hills
The road was built by white men for themselves
The road's a buffalo spear
hurtling from the lake,
wounded villages cling to its wake,
devouring the wind, the echo of drums, the green landscape.
The spearhead whetted with venom,
buries itself in the breast of Kampala
The mountains of the Moon
send rains to wash green dusty Christs

crucified on thorn trees and wild palms
And green popes nodding plumed heads of Royal Palms
excommunicate the wanton deities
of yellow acacia flowers, scarlet lilies
green foam of mangoes
and the siren smell of coffee blossoms.
Weep for the pride of presences gone
and the hope for the one who must return.

Who Pays the Piper?

Afterwards
they lay deep, deep in the trough of sunlight
silver sands and sea anemones,
seventy-eight mauled bodies
on altars of turquoise;
sea urchins clung to crushed rib cages;
and shrimp danced in eyeless sockets of skulls
cradled in coral and sea fans.
Flotation cushions sailed helter-skelter
towards an apoplectic Soufrière
whose cratered vomit promised
ever rising tides of molten magma;
others scudded before the wind
towards the magical Grenadines
until children and fishermen
gathered them like seaweed.
The assassins boasting in bulletins
from Miami were pipers of death
whose tune was bought before they played.

Faces and Skulls

Time pleats dark flesh
around white bones.
Time scrapes away my black face
And chiseling
a white skull appears.

Housewives in Dearborne

Housewives in Dearborne
Are buying guns
For a safari of black men
Women expecting to be raped
Discovering
An orgasm of guns.

The White Sun Dying

The white sun dying, dying
falling like a wounded crane
the white sun
leaning like a cruel conquistador
on lances of sunlight
The white sun
burning itself out like a comet
or a candle in a cave
the white sun
drowning
in an ocean of fire
The white sun singing, singing
singing the songs of the dead
the white sun
a burning requiem
but the coal night must come
The white sun
biting like a vaquero's whip.

Ashes and Silence

Our nuclearized world
finally wore a skin
of cinders, ashes and emptiness
in the aftermath
of the Pentagon's end game
the incense-scent of vaporized flesh
perfumed the hot, isotopic air
no witness but the wind
survived to tell the tale
of bodies Nagasakied
in typhoons of fire.
Shadows peopled pavements of leveled cities
dreaming spires had vanished
nothingness reigned
dust was memoryless
after evanescent pyrotechnics
had imploded the final breath of the living;
incandescent mushroom clouds
sheet lightninged
the stygian doomsday sky
laddering hell to heaven
storms of flame
calcined the Pearly Gates;
lovers of death shared funeral pyres
with heretics
Cantors, priests, charlatan shamans
politicians, more eloquent than satan,
preached vaingloriously
from lecterns of terror
of our planet earth's death by fire.
We perished, each of us,
a thousand times
as planners at the count-down
had ordained.
No leaves stirred,

No birds sang,
no babies cried.
In the beginning was the word
In the end ashes, cinders and silence.

Ballad for a Revolution

Grenada,
Spice Island to the windward
of the rising sun
Kaierouanne kept his word
The thunder axe
has struck a hammer blow
that's echoing across an archipelago
where dreams were curved and chained and lashed
and ancestors carried empires on their backs
Grenada,
Kaierouanne, Bishop, and Fedon
are dancing
To bongo beats of liberation drums
Caonabo is singing a poem hymn
Anacoana is shouting defiance at conquistadors
Fidel's repeating his prophesy
that when there is stirring
of the people's ire
tyrants go to sleep in power
and wake up in exile

Building the Great Wall

Basketeers carrying stones
with bruised hands
listening to crickets
slaves who had not paid their tribute in the feathers
or kingfishers, Meou tribesman bewildered
by distances of a journey to nowhere,
Southerners with frostbitten toes
dark Hindus with limpid eyes
Pathans bent like trees
Turks, Jews, Kazaks, Uzbeks, Tadjiks,
Koreans, Nipponese and beardless blacks
from islands south of the winter
dying in green winters
Captives of the Kha-Khans
Emperors in
palaces of the rising sun
casting shadows
on indifferent snows
as they strolled
in the golden lamp light
shadowless and jaded
with lust.

Vulcan Speaks

Canaries sang morning melodies
when Soufrière's rage
was all but spent.

My shafted heart was still
above the river's clamorous
murmurings.

The silent fury
of Ontario snows
hushed longings
in my heart.

When love dies
it vanishes
like Spring snows
in sun's blind and burning eye.

The dogs of war
never sleep
like rivers pregnant with
the heavy rains.

Grenada! Grenada!

to Roberto Retamar with fraternal greetings in this hour of trial

Grenada! Grenada!

You can betray this revolution
for a moment in time
but you can never
extinguish its fire

Burn fire, burn!
under folds of lava skin
that covers hills and glades
of defiance
it is the fire of volcano
hidden in chasmed hollows
of the heart and mind
Brother Bishop, Fidel, Daniel O,
they're trying to revile
a friendship forged
in fires of volcano
but the fire-seeds you garnered
in silos bursting with ideas
were scattered by a hurricane
the revolution lives!
You can betray the revolution
for a moment
but you can never extinguish its fire

Burn fire, burn.
The revolution lives!
Soufrière was erupting
In a neighbouring isle
The morning of a march day
When Brother Bishop said,
'Stand up, brothers and sisters,
and stretch limbs
cramped from too much kneeling,
this is a revolution for bread, for jobs,
for the liberty of the suffering folk,
stand up, I say,
and never kneel again!
Soufrière, echoed Brother Bishop's words,
with a declaration of fire
dimming the luminosity of night stars
They say that Soufrière's sleeping now
And Bishop's lying in a nameless grave
But can volcanic fires die?
You can betray the revolution
for a moment
But you can never extinguish its fire.

Burn fire, burn
The revolution lives!
Brother Bishop's voice
is cradled in a hurricane
And pounding like fists
inside the brains
of those who might despair:
'Stand up, brothers and sisters,
and stretch limbs
cramped from too much kneeling.
This is a revolution for bread, for jobs,
for the liberty of the suffering folk, stand up, I say
and never kneel again!'
The revolution lives!

Chicago, 15 December 1983

I Fight for What Must Be

I fight for what must be
For what is sometimes
stabs emptily like daggers in the wind
And yet there's beauty
in what is
Birdsong, sun, sea music.
I fight for what must be and memories that
cling like bark to a tree
And Sharpeville's ember burning
burning, burning
before the conflagration.

If He's Killed We'll Bleed

'People get trial and prison... and death while government get hearings and re-elections.'
Mumia Abu-Jamal, 12 July 1995

Brother Mumia Abu-Jamal said quietly
'Look and you'll see a widening politics of DEATH?
And MALCOLM's warning echoed from an untimely grave,
three decades away
'WHEN YOU BEGIN TO THINK, YOU FRIGHTEN THEM.'
Mumia had the malice to think aloud
and having thought his thoughts
he honed them from brain and tongue to pen
sounding wakeup calls
that burst like stardust
inside our heads.
That's why Grim Reapers
in robes and wigs, uniforms and Brooks Brothers vines
are hawking
Death on the installment plan
trying to amortize the human self that's him
and replicate Hitler's Parisian victory jig
celebrating corpses of innocents
vomited from the guts of other death rows
burgeoning jail cells
Death row
death watch
death pen-al-ty
reclaiming the streets
being tuff on crime
EUPHEMISMS FOR OFFICIAL MURDER
'unless it's their own'
Brother Abu-Jamal said;
'People get trial and prison...and death'
Murder for sale at the hustings
The in-justice system

spawns blood-seeds of Kali the Destroyer
chorusing Kill, kill, kill!
its death penalty song
is number one
on a macabre hit parade
in the White House
white, Doric-columned State Houses
white Mansions of Mayors
the obscene Court houses
the Capitol.
Kill, kill, kill,
warehouse the souls of Black and Latino folk
spin racist fantasies
and in particular,
silence this one,
a midnight man with an enchanted tongue
a truth-teller
defying the sowers of death
who sings of life
and mornings when sunrise will burnish
awakening eyes
We're tied to him with a blood-knot
flesh and sinew, bones and dreams
whirlpool inside
the same cauldron
of pain and hope
and ancestral resolution.
Let him live
for if he's killed
folks everywhere will bleed.

Letter to Agostinho Neto

Brother Neto,
Paloma mia, corazon.
I had to write
and call you by the fondest names
the way Blacks of the Diaspora do
to greet a comrade, banish pain.
Fighter from ramparts of Africa's flesh
the season of vampires fills me with dread
and I must pen anxious alarms.
I know that vampires have surrogates—
jackals black and white, ghouls who fear the New Day,
snakes with agile tongues, and carrion birds—
I'm certain that you're vigilant
morning, noon, and through the long nights,
but I must warn you just the same;
assassins never risk an open fight,
they come like thieves in daylight or the night
to steal a life.
They bound the enchantment of Lumumba's tongue
with lime and clinker from Katanga's mines;
his murderers are abroad again, beware!
I have a dream, an everlasting dream
that someday I'll return to Angola
and find the part of me that's waiting there
on the plains, in the forests
or the hills and mountains of home;
and if I don't find it in Angola
I'll walk south to the Cape or north
to El Jadida and the desert shores
and everywhere people will say:
'Your ancestors are here, you're home!'
Brother Neto, if you're too busy then
perhaps you'll ask a relative or friend
to walk with me and be my guide,
past mangrove and the wild green coast

and sand all golden in the afternoon
and when sea-drums resurrect echoes
louder than rhapsodies of pounding surf
maybe the wind with lisping tongues
might tell us of the day or night
my ancestor left Africa and home
naked and chained to oaken floors of sorrow.
Fighter from ramparts of Africa's flesh
the night of vampires must give way to day-clean,
warriors will return to long cool evenings
and the wine jars and the children
chanting poem-hymns and dancing.
Then I will follow roads like veins
to the anthracite heart of Africa
and everywhere people will shout
'Your ancestors are here, you're home!'

P.S.: If you're still wondering why I had to write
the reason is clear as bells or starlight,
'If they come for you in the morning,
they'll come for me that night.'

The Children are Dying Quietly

The children are dying quietly
like flies
but that's a slander
for Drosophila Melanogaster, the fruit fly
renews itself in ten to fifteen days . . .
No, the children are dying quietly
like desert flowers that once had bloomed
after the rain
before the vampire sun came back again
I saw one child of the hundred thousand
cradled in parched grass
a dusty acacia, rattling dry peas in pods
sounded like a magician's rattle
playing a requiem
and a hoarse, asthmatic wind
hollered in the nearby hills
where jackals slept
One child of the hundred thousand
with lemur eyes
staring at the sun
Children, grandparents, parents, neighbours and friends alike
in that order
are being rubbed out, erased from time and space

The Death of Lumumba

To die a lonely death
with only the echoes of voices, crying, Uhuru! Uhuru!
This was the fate of a dreaming man,
son of a warrior tribe – the Batatelas,
The tribe of all men crying, Uhuru! Freedom!
Out of the empty days, out of the lost years.
others have died but none so lonely:
None have known the agony of his last days
entombed in a sepulcre of hate,
journeying to the forest of the long night.
But tears have never warmed the cold hearts of the dead,
and I will raise my banner in the sorrowing winds
and shout.
This man and his comrades Mpolo and Okito
walked the green plains below the mountains of the Moon
and saw the sunsets on great rivers that the mountains fed –
the Congo, the Limpopo, the eternal Nile;
This brother who had spoken to a King
and was more royal than the Sons of Heaven
His pride was naked,
no vestments, no coronets, no lambent eyes, no vacant smiles,
No opiate of words to soothe his enemies
he rose up like a comet, burning out himself to light the world,
Black Africa has known no other in our time
Who left bright lightnings
so that dying there remains
an everlasting memory of light.
I must not weep for him
for mossy stones will weep
beside the lake in Kivu.
And if I weep my tears must fall like long rains
that herald the paths of thunder.
His final dream was this:
those who plunder and betray
must inherit the wild winds of my people's anger,

And I will reap the wind and share the harvest of my anger
with the world of living men.
In the wide continent of his vision
he sought to build a Republic of Freedom
This vision is my heritage
So tell me no more words about his dying,
no requiems on the singing drums,
no sakadas for him
For I will reap the wind and share my anger
with the world of living men.
An atrocious death, an unknown grave,
yet many feet will walk aslant green trails of memory
in pilgrimage.
How lonely the dead are!
And yet I will not weep for him,
I'll write no epitaph
but raise my banner high
PATRICE LUMUMBA! HERO! PATRIOT!
Too many hearts like talking drums
will beat the morse code of his martyrdom,
and tell of a man who talked to kings
and was more royal than the Sons of Heaven.
The Earth that mothered him, that mothered Africa
now binds the enchantment of his tongue.
But words he spoke remain:
Uhuru! Freedom!
And I will raise my banner high as clouds
that flank the burning sun:
PATRICE LUMUMBA! HERO! PATRIOT!

February, 1961

Tributes and Requiems

Tribute to Dobru

Dobru, dead?
No, never!
The double 'R' warbler
with Santigron in his blood
is with Boni and Abaisa
monsooning in Surinam
Dobru, the double 'R' warbler
Is doing a walk-about
with the stars
but when morning
cleans the motes of darkness
from Night's eye
you'll always find him
grounding with Boni doro and Abaisa
at Brokopondo
where the raging white water
is a mirror-image
of their tiger-orchid grins.
Dobru, the double 'R' warbler
has slipped away
up the Gran Rio;
he and Boni and Abaisa
are palavering
at Tapawatara,
pouring libations to the Old Ones
while the river's a symphony of white water

Chicago, March 1984

For Buzz

Buzz
Thank you for laughter
that filled our hearts with a particular gladness
after overwhelming odds forced us to retreat
That laughter, too, lifted our spirits high as stars
when we won victories.
Too soon, too soon the years have spun
their tangled skeins of passing time!
Seven decades? Seventy years!
But is there a continent or island
that your vision has not encompassed?
Sparks of memory have ignited
Eternal legacies of hope
And you have taught us to exorcise
Abysmal glooms of buried fears,
The poison darts hurled at you
from integrated towers –
ebony, ivory and brown - are proof
that empty vessels make the most noise
You were not daunted
By the terror and the time
So let the freedom bells ring and ring again
for your seventieth year!

Lost Steps I Found, II

for Alejo Carpentier

I found lost steps
to my motherland's heart
under her green untidy flesh;
veined rivers mapped
the wanton circumference
of her loins,
her belly-skin
trembling,
like surfaces of still water under the wind,
her bosoms
higher than Akarai hills,
the steep descent into her womb
threatening mysteries
of Kamarian ravines,
her eyes
sun-kissed wells
guarding depths
of mirth and hurt
and wildest longings.
The lost steps
to my motherland's heart
lead to my Pakaraimas
and Roraima of the Red Rock
the ever fertile source of streams
where ferns and flowers
reach to touch my face,
and dreaming roots and sleeping snakes
would bar my way.
The lost steps
in Amazonian Palaces to the Sun
where rivers speak
like talking drums,
and everlasting winds

hum litanies,
and listening,
I'm certain that I hear
my own voice echoing
through arching narthexes
of amarata trees.

Tribute to Claudia

Commemorating 50 years since she founded the West Indian Gazette

Claudia Jones was soft-spoken in her social conversations, but her voice could ring out and fill a crowded auditorium when she was making a public speech. The last time I heard her speak in public was when she introduced Paul Robeson at a rally in the St. Pancras Town Hall. This meeting was a fundraiser for Claudia's community newspaper, the *West Indian Gazette*. I do not remember any instance when Claudia raised her voice in the course of a conversation. There was a Trinidadian politeness in the way in which she listened to the person, or persons, to whom she was speaking. She was a mixture of the Trinidadian, the Afro-American, and the woman of the world, but despite the softness in her demeanor, she could be very persuasive. I remember one of her countrymen telling me, 'Claudia can persuade you to do something, and you will go away believing it was your decision and yours alone.' She kept the *West Indian Gazette* alive against almost impossible odds. When her illustrious friends like Paul Robeson and W.E.B. Du Bois visited London, she got them to appear at rallies for the paper. Those who knew her also knew about her heart condition, and that she was living on borrowed time. She wore the mantle of greatness which she carried around with her with ease and dauntless courage. And she never faltered in the exemplary choices that she had made. She was a Black woman, a Caribbean woman, a woman of international renown, and up to her last day on this Mother Earth of ours, she fought the good fight. Claudia, rest in peace. We will never forget you.

Tribute to My Mother

The Chinese say
that women hold up half the sky
but my mother who's witnessed
changing seasons of nights and days
for a hundred years
declares
'we are the fulcrum
balancing earth and sky,
the magic weavers
on the looms of life
and finally we must decide
if the breast of the earth
suckles new generations
or withers and dies.
We must decide.'
My mother spoke
inside the echo chamber of eternal memories
Her fight was not for equality
but for the right to decide
the fate of the mothering earth
her echo chamber was the universe
she had an inner ear for harmonies
of stars and galaxies
circling
the muted rage
of those banished
to islanded outposts
outside the human race
My mother of a hundred years
was called Amai, the Earth Mother,
The One Who Must Decide
She was Nanny
leading a nation of maroon fighters
on the long, impossible march
to Trelawny

She was Gamay, fighting side by side
with Fedon
unfurling with a song
the slogan
Liberty or Death!

Poem for a Boy of Nine Who Left Us

for Badi and Juanita and Nabil

A manchild scythed
by the Grim Reaper's random choice of lives
leaves hearts splintered
and hurts too deep, too deep for telling
The Grim Reaper came in broad daylight
forfeiting four score years
and one,
hurrying the morning
of his days
into chasms
of eternal night,
his awakening must live
inside our hearts like sparks
striking the flint of our patience
our everlasting faith.
And yet the mystery of death
The coffin'd grief
bites deep
too deep for tears
or telling.
Listening
we hear again his laughter
and starlighted our waiting.
He glistened like a seal
and cried for life, more life,
and yet
nine years was his allotted time
nine years!
Too soon, too soon
he crossed the Rubicon
leaping away quite suddenly
through an exit of death.
We clutch at memories

of laughter, golden days, scolding, tears
and things he said
when listening
we did not really hear.
But with his dying
his voice is sunrise
in echo chambers of our glooms,
he teaches us again
the patient mysteries of listening
to children,
dying he bequeathed to us
a heritage of love
as tender as his breath
when he was sleeping.
The day that quiet Gospeller
whispered his name
from pulpits in the Autumn skies
the call was too gentle
for our listening ears
and now
the arched trajectory of pain
haunts, and hurts
like hatpins in the brain.
A boy of nine
innocent of death
as cassia flowers
trapped in eternal Spring
has left us.
The day he went away
dawned
and would have waxed and waned
like any other
except the numbing news
stabbed and exploded
the pain drip, dripped
there were no echoes in the emptiness
no leaves stirred
no birds sang

we dredged from unplumbed chasm'd depths
the will to live for him
and for a pluriverse of children.
He's gone to walk among the stars
walk well in peace in love.

Amherst, 13 November 1976

For Syl

She slipped away quietly
one morning during the long rains
her last breath came just like a sigh
and then she slept so deeply that
they couldn't awaken her
Her face is no longer at the window
when I pass by and her sweet smile's only a memory.
Her conversations with her priest
must now take place in paradise
and yet I wish she were still here
to visit on cool afternoons
Her life was never very great
but it was honest, and when she wept tears
they fell upon her starched blouse
like benedictions for others.
She slipped away so quietly
I'm sure she's where she wants to be
with dogs and flowers and her priest
in gardens of eternity.

Requiem for Ted Watkins

Red the heart and red the enchanted tongue
the flowers blooming on his chest were red
the bullets plant red roses in pastures of black flesh
and myrtles on his brow turn red,
poppies are red
and red peonies are a black man's heart.
The master of the Day of Doom called out his name:
Ted Watkins! He came to the edge of the
forest of the Long Night, and danced to the music of drums
and flutes
running with fire for feet
Black Wendigo! Avenger!
Come back to the drums and flutes of home.
The red moon spans the Middle Passage,
names
of black princes and paupers alike
are inscribed on papyrus scrolls
that roll with the wild sea tides
until they find a couch to sleep
tangled in the long red hair of Sargasso sirens.
Africa, America
replete with the drums that spoke ancestors' names
a hundred thousand tides ago…
Ancestor, Atta, Otu, Krumah, Acara, Antar,
the names were erased
he recalled them, bellowing
at the mouth of caves of lost centuries…
red the stars, and red the eyes of fireflies
circling the Forest of the Long Night
red the necklace of bonfires.
The Master of the Day of Doom called once again,
Called out, Ted Watkins!
Lord of black heavens and white hells,
The merciful one, the redeemer
My name's on a papyrus Sargasso scroll

Wrapped around bones of Shango princes.
Lumumba, of the Batatela Tribe, my brother.
Son of Boshongo Kings,
Nkrumah, of the Enzemas, my cousin,
My clan, the Dagambas,
And Ibos were my enemies
Until I married in the tribe the Ijaw woman,
Hunters, from the Niger
Walk with me to the Mountains of the Moon to meet
my kith and kin,
and the Herero herdsmen taught me
to repeat this incantation to red galaxies
'the earth that mothered us, that mothered Africa
breeds no barbarians no strangers anywhere'
red his eyes and red his breast
a thousand red roses blooming on his chest.
He stumbled into the forest of the Long Night
And, reeling through a gauntlet of flame-flowers
he heard meadowlarks sing requiems low
the forest of the long night is black,
his heart is forever red.

Requiem for Andrew

Andrew, Andrew, the diaries
recording your journeys to Havana and Georgetown
meticulously, are closed,
Malcolm Heartland is home at last.
You kept the faith
and never joined the sam-fye dance
of those who wheeled and turned
and did the B'ra Anancy prance with words.
You were a truth-teller, a scholar-man,
a poet troubadouring your way through labyrinths
searching for light
The Quality of Violence that you penned
calcined our universal hurts
Malcolm Heartland is home
but the last stanzas of his poem-hymn
are open ended and waiting
for new maestros to orchestrate
the music and the singing.
Andrew, Andrew, there are so few of us left
the boon companion days
at Notting Hill and Moscow Road
are filtering like Stardust
through a sieve of lowering skies,
yet I remember well that only yesterday
we were reveling in heresies
celebrating the dreams
of Bogle, Marti, Garvey, Che, Bishop, Fedon
and the incomparable Fidel;
denouncing the fractured vision of a Caribbean
surfing in mirages of market economies;
Yes, we made mirth of Yeltsin's treacheries.
and remembered how
the wily Talleyrand
had once declared
that 'treason is a matter of timing,'

in conversations spanning half a century
we talked about our peers
and how, the malice of our homeland was
harder to endure than exile
to raging silences of winter snows
Andrew, Andrew,
How blithe was your spirit!
How generous your heart!
And those you helped, Ah, so many!
Their gratitude, alas, was not unlike
the borealis race of Robbie Burns's poem,
'that flits e're you can point its place'.
It was blossomtime in the Amherst Spring
when Malcolm Heartland checked out
and headed home
and now they're excavating dusty laurel wreaths
with which to crown him
but he's escaped and towers over them
feet on the earth
and head in the stars
he's laughing now
and singing
his unrepentant and melodic poem-hymns.

Lincoln University, 4 May 1995

Requiem for My Sister

Using the tragedy of my sister's death to call for racial harmony in Guyana.

I sent no flowers for her dying,
the withered petals fall into the dust too soon;
The earth that mothered her
will offer blossoms to the sun again,
Bluebells and wild azaleas
Down paths of thunder at Ichillibar
Not long ago I saw the pain deep in her eyes,
the bite of splintered bones, and daggers in the brain.
Those eyes had searched my own and asked a reason for her dying,
I did not know the answer, and I lied…
My heart was blind,
and tears were muted orisons.
I could have told her,
the votaries are constant,
Death holds dominion in the Kingdom of the Dead;
veined rivers in the brain will flow no more
When kokers stem tides of anguish;
the Pastures of Heaven are no longer green,
they wear marmoreal colours,
And flowers sculpted in stone
resist wailing requiems in the wind…
Memories are monuments,
eyeless granite draped in adamantine shrouds.
She lies where the living world wears green,
and there, some part of me is buried,
A magic seed,
waiting for rains to come like a benediction.
We shared a childhood in the land we loved,
the land of our beginning,
our first lullaby, our first singing.
The land of our first enchantment,
our pristine laughter, and idle tears;

When we bent moonbeams with awkward hands,
out of lost centuries, came,
myths of gods and devils –
Duppy, massa-kruman;
mermaids singing their siren songs;
Kanaima, stalking men in forests of the night;
Anancy with his agile brain;
The Pi-ai-man, performing his demoniac rites,
The Kalimai Priest
chanting a liturgy of song-poems
murmuring his prayers;
We were inheritors of a land
from Waini Point to Akarai,
from Orealla to Roraima.
But seasons brought their drought and flood,
we saw the parched earth thirsting for rains,
wide savannahs, cracked and veined;
people, twisted like limbs of saman trees…
Only the croton in our garden survived,
its varnished leaves with yellow traceries,
defied the sun.
The other flowers died.
Bodies were hollow logs of bone,
the skin stretched tight as a drum.
But cinders deep inside our famished hearts
ignited into flame
We were the heirs of everlasting hope;
The dream that all peoples have a right to share
the waters of the River of Life,
and drink with their own cups,
Was one I nourished, felt it germinate;
My sister taught me how to guard this dream;
She taught me that the colour of a man
was not a dye that marked the skin,
The colour really flashed
in the kaleidoscope of his imaginings!
And when the final reckoning came
a man was as much as his shadow

as much as his love.
My sister loved the land, and stayed,
I went on endless journeyings.
wandering through cities
with their monuments in stone,
And I, an exile from myself,
walked in the wide indifference
of sun-less sepulchers,
where age is worshipped, and age is the worshipper.
The memory of home
is like the bread of life to those who roam,
Home is a speck upon the spinning globe
where finally the earth
will fill the hollows of the skull,
bind the enchantment of the tongue.
Some memories are moored
beyond the whirlpools and the changing tides.
Where harbours of home are locked by the land.
forgotten secrets live inside
The songless echoes of the singing drums,
or grow like orchids,
high in the forests of the flesh.
My sister kept those memories for me...
but Death came suddenly,
Mantop, walked in sunlight,
and darkness fell at noon.
I know the land is stained with blood;
Guns speak. The answering echoes die.
Bullets are marked with innocent names,
and madness skulks in the uneasy glooms.
Guns only speak in monotones of death,
and victims stagger stupidly,
fall and fuse with their shadows.
Rage lights new bonfires
in hearts of the bereaved.
How many victims can one dead man claim?
This is a time when mockingbirds sing,
but no one answers, no one hears.

Who-you birds count heads at night
and moonlight lies upon living shadows
Like a lover.
Faceless ghosts gather under silk cotton trees,
phantoms of no race, colour, no creed!
Atta and Akara, stand side by side with Ayub and Kai;
those marked with crosses on the breast
were once the masters;
They bellow orders in the night,
but no one answers, no one cares.
The other races, too, are there,
huddled shoulder to shoulder, pressing close,
a ring of lonely ghosts
around the gnarled and ancient trees,
speaking in many tongues,
But all ghosts sound like hummingbirds,
stitching holes in moonlit air.
The who-you birds call out the names.
The ranks are packed.
Two headless men came down the dusty road,
voices issued from flutes stuck in their gory throats,
their voices were the same.

'We've come to join the Brotherhood of the Dead!' they cried.
'We've no place for headless men', the who-you birds replied.
The ghosts filed past in twos and threes,
their hollow laughter echoed everywhere,
and blossoms fell like snow upon their heads.
The headless men fluted sad songs like sadakas,
until the last ghost disappeared
climbing a ladder of moonbeams.
I must return to the land of my fathers
to claim the dreams my sister kept for me.
I'll make a pilgrimage to her grave,
and every tear I shed will be
for all the nameless dead who died in vain – the innocents.
Their judges and their executioners were the same,
Caesar and God were one.

Scorpions can sting themselves to death, not men!
We must mark the New Day with forests of wild flowers;
weave new garments out of starlight...
Clothed in stars, and armed with ragged dreams,
the poor must walk erect and tall,
and seize a place with God.
The ghosts of slaves
will never cease their sorrowing at night
until dark sentinels
with bare hands and bare feet
tear asunder pale ramparts of heaven,
to pluck wild orchids of ultimate release.
One day, the wind over the canfields must sing, not sigh.
Sweet incense from gum of Acacia trees
Must banish the stench of blood.
We're all our Brothers' keepers.
Let no one dare to rob us of this heritage.
Gnawing at bones of everlasting griefs,
caught in the thrall of masters and slaves,
Ours is a legacy of love and hate,
love for the living, hate for the living dead.
Compassion's chiseled deep inside our skulls,
so set the prisoners free, open the jails!
We'll judge the innocent and guilty for ourselves
First we must call the judges to the bar, the magistrates,
And ask, 'Who buys the piper's tune before he plays?'
When guilty men are free, and innocents are chained,
then all the people in our land are prisoners.
The hatred of ourselves bites deep,
leaves us with wounds that will not heal.
Those with cramped limbs stiff from too much kneeling,
suffer a vertigo when they stand up straight.
Those who deny their heritage, die the first death.
The other death is like a play,
where mourners sing around an empty grave.
My sister lies beyond my reach.
She's buried where the living world wears green.
Roots of wild flowers

will guard the shattered casements of her heart.
But the dreams we shared are safe.
I must return to the land of my forefathers to inherit them.

Requiem for Cheddi Jagan

The river, amber-tinted by drenching rains,
garlands the falling tide with water hyacinths
and sings requiems for him on his way home
to ricefields and savannahs and bitter-sweet
sugarcane
where refrains of suffering still echoed in the wind
and streams veining forests and a maracage
flowed in time to the rhythms of rebellious hearts.
They laid him to rest on a funeral pyre
and north-east Trades
gusting down corridors of Atlantic tides
touched his embalmed face
while lashing winds and rain
transformed prayer flags to Shiva
into red banners of his pristine dream
that the torment of the poor and despised
must be redeemed forever.
His eyes were closed
the orisons of priests
echoed across plumed arrows of the canefields
but showers of sparks rained down upon the mourners
reminding them
that deep inside the swaddling cotton shroud
was a dauntless heart of fire
and fire is never timid when it bonds with the winds of time.
Riversong and windsong
rhythms of rain
drumming on his funeral pyre
and a Swami and his acolytes cantoring poem-hymns
sang requiems for him at Port Mourant and home.
But showers of sparks and burning embers
fanned by an insurgent wind
deluged the bereaved, warning them
that hearts of fire never rest in peace
that embers hissing in the rain

can always burst into flame again and again
and leap as high as stars.
When a host of mourners melted in the mothering dark
the fire's glow brightened the night
and starlight jewelled dewdrops on petals of wild flowers,
a watchman of dayclean swore
that ancestor Acabre had come
in the witching hour
to greet a kindred spirit of fire.
'Look out for them,' the watchman said,
'from this day onwards,
the two, ever vigilant,
with their fearless mothers beside them
will walk hand-in-hand from Waini Point to Akarai
Orealla to Roraima
I tell you, they'll make sure
that we unite
to realize their undying dreams.'

Louisville, March 1997

On Visiting Phillip Agee

He was trapped in Hamburg
caged in his apartment
that was a ten minute walk from Am Weiher.
Even when he was quiet,
you could hear
high tension wires
singing inside his head.
He had made a manicheistic choice
And was paying for it
in a currency of anguish.
We talked about sailing from Grenada
to Carriacou
in the blue-green Caribbean.
perhaps it was cruel reminiscing
The way we were,
for those he had exposed remorselessly
with a peculiarly upright courage
would never forgive him
they wanted him dead and silenced
because they sensed that his ideas,
with their diamond-hard cutting edge,
would endure
beyond the immediacy of their venom.
We talked about schooners, fishing boats,
Hurricanes and sails
that reveled in the wind's pleasure.
There was tenderness,
raw pain,
and the schoolboy's smile on his face
as I walked away
carrying a slice
of his Gethsemane
out of the door.

Requiem for My Auntie

My auntie died
five days before
her ninety-second birthday
She did not
slip away quietly
she fought
for more life.
Odds never daunted her
she wanted to decide
on the time and place
In her imperious way
she had to take
the initiative
with this final decision
and neither
God nor man
could take
this privilege away from her.
She'd lost
her speech
and her eloquent hands
were silent
all that was left
was an invincible heart
and eyes
asking questions.
A smile on her pale lips
acknowledged my presence
She was handing me
the fallen standard
that was ripped apart
by time and the wind.

Requiem for the Innocent

Wanted
Dead or alive
for a murder
and a multitude of crimes
A creature, armed, desperate, dangerous
a creature wearing
a humanoid disguise
Usually carries a calling card
touting freedom, democracy,
free enterprise.
Yesterday, Wednesday, the sixth,
it assassinated
seventy-eight innocents
in emerald seas
off Barbados.
And across the lees
of two continents
in Thailand.
Hundreds of the young
were mowed down
by its unconscionable hand.
Two thousand million others
are dying in twilight vales
of starvation
Where its surrogates
Princes, Prelates, Pimp-Presidents,
Buccaneers of profit
are looting labour and life.
The victims live
a strobe light flash in time,
averaging twenty-seven years
or counting by moons
three hundred and twenty-eight.
Wanted
Dead or alive

for Murder, Ethnocide, Mayhem,
Racism and the rape
of continents, islands
skies and seas
Imperialism
a creature armed, desperate, dangerous.

Requiem for Warren

He did not 'go gentle into his long night'
instead, 'he raged against the dying of the light....'
He walked a trail straight as an arrow's flight
and was a lifelong enemy of compromise.
When Mantop stole into a sanctum of his inner life
to menace him
their eyes made four
but as of yore
he turned to bosom friends
and proffered a convivial toast
disguising wrenching fears
and the mute, tormenting pain
of an imminent and final parting
In the meantime,
soothing evenings
slipped stealthily into night
for the longest year since calendars recorded time.
During this borrowed time,
his mind, swift as a streak of light
grasped spoken things and things unsaid alike.
With wit and an urbane aplomb
he proved more often than I care to count
that *in vino veritas* was a canon,
not a punster's jibe.
He's gone to walk amongst the stars
still, I can picture him
measuring the elegant, comet-bright curve
between Canis Major and a rosette Mars
and recording with characteristic precision
a factor of ten plus a dreamtime of infinity.
He did not 'go gentle into his long night'
instead, he 'raged against the dying of the light.'

Requiem for Vernon

Vernon
although earth and ashes
now bind the enchantment of your tongue
I can still hear your voice inside my head
Telling me tales of salad days in Tennessee
Laughter came as easily
as water singing in a brook
to spice the Jim Crow episodes.
There was underneath
those laughter-ridden tales
A will of steel, a timeless dedication
bolstered by a mother's voice
a grandmother's admonitions
You heeded their advice
and used words like assegais
Following Neruda's dictum
that metaphors are powerful weapons in the fight
for love, human rights, and liberty
Vernon
the muted mesmeric rhythms of your voice
telling me tales
with an avuncular ease
of salad days
and ways of sunlight and shadow
echo inside my head
like Easter bells.
When you decided to pick up
the fallen standards
you must have heard
ancestral voices chanting poem hymns
telling in soft cadences
that our promised land
is for all except
the meek or the poor in spirit.
Vernon

you taught a younger generation
that a mind equipped with knowledge
can scale Olympian heights.
Vernon
you discovered long ago
that apportioning blame or praise to skin colour
was a fraudulent melanin game
that ignored the treasure trove
of human diversity
You knew that in the final reckoning
every human being
was as much as their shadow
as much as their love.
And finally walking across shadows and light
you discovered that the best
of writing and music and scholarship
must always be like lightning
for lightning illuminates
and is never afraid.
Go well my brother
walk across shadowless daylights
and nights infested with stars

Louisville, 31 October 2004

For Martin Carter

If I could write with fire
pure fire
I, too, would burn
incinerate
calcine
the lies
I tell myself
and the lies I live.
And some of those
I face
each day
conversing
in my well-bred way
I'd hurl my words at them
like assagais
to mutilate
or else
I'd place upon their heads
spiked crowns
to exorcise
my treachery and theirs
watching
blood
tie shoelaces
under their chins
if I could write with fire
I'd die
rather than compromise
with them
and be
the inheritor
of Malcolm's
awakening
and Toussaint's dream.
If I could write with fire

pure fire
I'd burn this city down
and write my poem
with drums
and dancing flames.

Louisville, December 1997

The Guyanese Wanderer

Before Majorca

Wandering man
are you frontiering
to new importunate destinations
are you horizon crashing
to mirages of green pastures
are you troubadouring again
to Berlin in the Autumn
and memories gusting
like leaves before the wind;
to Hamburg where reluctant Springtimes
court capricious summers
To London and the plane trees on Regent's Square
or to Wiggen Hall St. Mary's the Virgin,
my daughter's castle in the air
Will you hie
to keening cacophonies of trains and planes
and cars careening
down mirrored highways after the rains?
Is there some Carib nomad strain
drip-dripping in your blood?
Did ancestors cross wild Sargasso seascapes
and caravel to forced labour in a new world?

Amherst, 27 May 1986

Prague Revisited

My face,
had
beaten against thirty-five years,
when I returned
but the city was the same,
chained to the Vltava
by elegant bridges.
Dreaming spires
still brooded by the mill-race,
Kafka's virtual castle
was a postcard silhouette
against purpling skies.
Pale sunlight
touched
Gilded baroque towers
And Jan Hus' beard
Still glittered fiercely
After a snowfall.

1985

Berlin

After a long cool summer
autumn winds descended from the mountains
and blowing helter skelter
made their way down
the severed Unter den Linden
and soft as a snowfall
entered the Brandenburg Gate
and soon autumn tinted leaves
The Siamese twin cities of Berlin
bisected by a wall
is limbo-ed in the midst
of lakes and meadows and trails for walkers
It beckoned me,
a wandering Carib troubadour,
to sing
about my distant world;
and I remember gusty afternoons,
when wind like filed teeth biting
into my dark flesh
ambushed me
at canyoned crossroads.

Exile (Toronto)

November was a dreaming month
when the monotonies of wide blue skies
brought to each day an insane ease.
The sunwheel danced around
eyeless sunflowers, yellow daisies,
flambeaux with stamens like parched tongues
purple anemones, and bumble bees
leeching pollen from chaliced flowers.
November was the month
when sea-drums echoed in my blood again.
And Clarky wrote,
'Dear Jan, Canada's cold, my friend,
and lonely sometimes like canaries
serenading jumbies in hell;
but there's bread . . .
and Philistines from home can't reach you here.'
It was the season when
curlews thronged southern skies
winging their clamorous way to ripening corn
and harvestime on the golden Pampas.
So I replied: 'Dear Clarky, as I write
the sunwheel's dallying over saffron swamps
on my Berbician coast;
marching crabs jewel the mud;
and herons hurl themselves
like flaming arrowheads
at the approaching night.
Why must I leave the sun
for timeless miseries of winter fog!'
And Clarky wrote again:
'You can't eat sun or drink the lazy tides
rimming your moon-burnished mud;
besides the pygmies and the philistines
multiply, become a host
when hardtime's knocking at your door,

their malice is much harder to endure
than silent furies of Ontario snows.
The people, yes, the people are all right,
but trapped in dreaming torpors of slow time.
Awaken them or leave, my friend!'
I replied, 'Awaken the people?
our awakening will come
when a maelstrom of pain
drives us outside the crumbling bastions
of our crippled selves;
when the New Day arrives
with morning flashing like sheet lightning
from our eyes;
together, side by side,
we'll burst asunder
pale ramparts of heaven
with bare hands and bare feet
and pluck wild orchids
of ultimate release.'

Return to Chicago

Tunnelling through clouds
piled up like dirty pillows
the 747 trembled
before touching down
I returned to Chicago's windy autumn
and had forgotten
in the southern sun
the Almighty Hawk
waiting outside the terminal
to greet me.
Its cold beak
touched my naked neck
And leaves scampered
at my feet
with rusty murmurings
The hawk's beak
heralded
my forty-fifth winter
promising
no mercy.

An Autobiography of Wandering

Berlin

Tell me, o can you tell me
what am I doing here
in this Siamese twin city
severed across its main artery
at the Brandenburg Gate
what am I doing here pardners and friends
liming off Martin Luther Strasse
on early autumn days
when I walk to the park by the waterworks
to watch young mothers
wheeling pink moon-faced children
in folding chairs
and old ladies leading miniature, castrated dogs
with immaculately tailored pelts
and claws manicured in smart beauty shops off the
Kauferdamn
salons for ladies of the
night and day and other pets
and similar shops for men
who hang out at street corners
waiting for a chance to dispel
an hour or two of loneliness
for a price –
pets holding human beings on a leash
leading them to an expectation of love
that is not there
around the pond's limpid eye
are children throwing crumbs
to indifferent, sated ducks
in autumn sunshine that's as cold
as memories of a home that after fifty years
of a nomad's journeying became
a speck upon the spinning globe,

a punctuation mark on a vast papyrus
chronicling
my Carib impulse to migrate
I stroll in a park of sated ducks, sated children, manicured hounds of hell
and women with hooded eyes
that occasionally make four with mine
revealing in a flash
abysses of unfulfilled desire
as if the eyes recognize in me,
perhaps mistakenly,
a barbarian
forever watchful, on the *qui vive*
one who inherited, along with a dark skin,
black magic to bleach and to invade
new frontiers of passion
shattering the lethargy of their waiting
storming expectations of unrequited longing
I leave the park and return to my apartment
on the Berchtesgadener strasse
I walk past the ruined church in the city centre
With a gilded clock face –
like a whore using theatrical make-up to disguise a shattered visage –
monument to a storm of bombs
and death by fire
I stroll down a street where trees
have not yet achieved the height
of old apartment buildings
I reach my flat and there
it is twilight at noontime
until I switch on the light in the passage
and I no longer feel that I am tunneling inside a labyrinth
What am I doing here listening to leaves
scraping along autumn pavements
before the lashing wind sends them scurrying
away from my feet
only yesterday, it seems,

there were tall linden trees
lining the streets and swaying
in the fall winds
like dancers with imprisoned feet
I walk past the ruined church in the city centre
and its gilded clock face smiled wickedly
uttering a hoarse mid-morning chime at eleven
the smile's a harlot's one
trying to disguise a ravaged visage
What is this monument for?
I ask myself
Is it a monument deploring Hitler's racial fantasies?
or, praising Red Liberators
and at the same time to remind those who would forget
allied bombings and death of a city by fire
I walk down streets where there's a
melancholy tale of a city's death by fire
when a storm of bombs had silenced
the laughter and crying of children
and the singing of wrens and nightingales?
Or is this mutilated spire
a finger pointing at God and reprimanding him
for his indifference to the death of millions.

Geneva

Geneva's clean
sanitized,
Calvin's hypocrisy
skulks behind
facades of opulence
But its emerald lake
festers
like a purulent belly button
islanded
in voluptuous flesh,
Bankers dine and dicker
over vintage wines,
paté de foie gras
and gilded desserts
But the youth of Geneva riot
exploding out of the wide indifference
that would hobble their lives
with a surfeit of plenty.

17 June 1980

Cuba

Ten Years: 1959-1969

Ten years have slipped by
since the imperishable deeds
of Fidel, Camilo and Che
have rocked the world
and changed relationships
between oppressor and oppressed
ten years and Spartacus
has sprung to life again
echoes of his eloquent and persuasive voice
are calling on gladiators
to bound out of their cages
and shatter the myth
of Rome's invincibility.
Listening we also hear
once again
nostalgic ballads
with rhythmic beats
that gladiators sang
when they reached
the wind-swept harbour of Brindisi
we can still picture them
waiting impatiently
on the shores of the wine dark sea
bargaining with merchants, slippery as eels.
Who would betray them to crucifixion
along the Apian Way.
Blood dripping
at the foot of Spartacus' cross
exploded out of pods of time
and scattered
longings for liberty
like blossoms in the wind
the blossoms touched Toussaint's heart
Standing under a Saman tree
and with a sea of ebony faces around him

he could smell treachery in the air
so holding a rifle
high above his head
he testified
this is your freedom!

I speak, tonight,
from the
heartland of a hemisphere
where the daytime sun
refuses to abdicate
its suzerainty of summer skies.
While we were sleeping
Cuba was awake
and Borealis lights
were dancing
along the rim
of arctic horizons.
It was as if
the elements
were ignoring
different zones of time
and celebrating
the victories
of Fidel, Camilo, and Che.
Ten years,
and now
the celebration is world wide
On this tenth year of the Cuban revolution
an orchestra of northern lights
beguiles us
to dance and sing
to commemorate ten years
of a revolution
that changed the world.
Ten years,
and our world is the third,
the human world.

Across the blue green Caribbean sea
the living world
wears green Amazonian tapestries.
Toussaint died, betrayed,
in the fortress of Joux,
the cold fortress of Joux.
Christophe and Dessalines
were deaf to his pleas
for unity
but Bolivar heard him.
At Boyacá, the Liberator
burnt his boats
and the memory of
five defeats, spiraled in scarves of smoke.

Rain-frogs still converse with the moon,
and cicadas sing liberty songs.
Where Bolivar spat a clinker of Dragon's Teeth
and warriors sprung up
to free a continent.
Nat Turner, listening to small talk
at his master's table,
heard that Bolivar had declared that
'It is easier to plough the sea
than to rob the brave of their liberty.'
Nat Turner left a legacy
for John Brown, Owen,
Copeland, Kaggi,
and Emperor Green
this dauntless band of fighters
turned the arsenal at Harper's Ferry
into a pulpit
from which to sound
the knell against slavery
and to prove for all time
that the dream of freedom never dies.
Marx, Engels, Lenin, Mao, Ho Chi Minh
led a thousand million followers

down paths of thunder;
the reverberation of their marching feet
shook the world.
Marti awakening left a testament for Fidel
He chronicled immortal longings
and added new pages
to the Book Of The Universe
Ten years, and
echoes of singing drums,
tell of Garvey and Fidel
Malcolm and Fidel
Lumumba and Fidel
Ten years.
Come Back Africa, Asia, America,
Free!
Our Caribbean
jade archipelago,
islands garlanded
with sun-silvered beaches
jewelled stepping stones squeezed between
twin continents
Thousands of leagues
North to the Canadian Barrens
and South to Patagonia
of the strong winds
homeland of the legendary children of the sun
where tortured dreams
live side-by-side
with immortal longings
and monumental cruelties
Where rhythms are conjured up
to gird the world
with untrammelled melodies
Revolution is a river
that sweeps Augean stables clean.
Lest we forget,
it brings back a host of memories.
Do you remember, Cuba?

The cruel seasons
during that not too distant time?
when the New Year
came to Saigon, Hue
two hundred cities, hamlets, towns?
Tet was a season of awakening.
when we greeted the New Year
with garlands and guns.
Tet was a season when
maidens shedding leis
wore a necklace of grenades.
Brothers of the New Year everywhere
carry storms in famished hearts
following Spartacus, Toussaint, Bolivar,
Marx, Engels, Lenin, Mao, Ho,
Marti, Fidel, Camilo and Che
Do you remember Cuba?
When black folks were denied
the right to promenade in lazy ease
on golden beaches
or touch the sea's white foam with bare feet?
That's only a dismal memory today,
for Cuba is free.
Ten years!
Forever!

Cuba – Angola

the Slave Ancestor

The griots are alive!
Our everlasting rememberers
are chanting history again:
Cuba – Angola
Angola – Cuba
Havana – Luanda
Luanda – Havana
The blood-knot was tied
with ligaments of pain
on sea lanes where caravels had plied
since Cristobal had named his price
and Isabella had paid.
The griots sing softly of slave ships
hurrying before the Trades
ferrying cargoes
to destinations of sorrow –
a host of ebony people from the sun
buried alive
in heaving darkness of ships' holds,
listening for two months or more
to rhythms of sea-drums oscillate
between a lilt of sadness
and crescendos of rage.
The griots sing about a Captain,
who, blind to golden seascapes of Sargasso,
wrote in his log:
'The bodies of twelve negroes
were delivered to Atlantic deeps today.
Before the journey's end
we'll send at least three dozen more
to join them in their watery graves.'
Ten million nameless ones,
the chanted requiem claims,

were scattered in a boiling wake
of sharks and blood.
Survivors of the crossing,
blinded by an alien sun, staggering,
falling over their iron chains,
rocking from side to side on roots of pain,
huddled at last in harsh shadows
of El Moro's battlements.
Mulatto tallymen, with whips and straws,
counted heads, giving a nomenclature
of numbers, and tribes:
Anang, Ibibo, Ngombes, Wolofs, Angolans!
Boshongos, Hausas, Ewes, Angolans!
Fantis, Dagambas, Bembas, Angolans!
Ovimbundus, Ashantis, Angolans!
Kings, Queens, and serfs, griots and basias, healers,
priestesses, prophets, goldsmiths, warriors,
Paramount Chiefs, marabouts, gravedigger-priests,
Amazon bodyguards, witches, minstrels,
sacred and secular drummers, artisans
Cantors in the courts of kings, cavalrymen,
Smiths, farmers, traders, poets, artists, scribes,
All designated as negroes,
A single branding iron erased their identity.
Our griots end each stanza chanting
'Night will pass, day-clean will come!'

1980

The High Road to Harar

for Roberto Retamar

I'll take the high road to Harar again,
the Freedom Road,
and walk past dusty Dire Dawa in the morning
just after the rains
when the verging sand is littered with wild flowers
and the thorn trees are green.
I'll hurry down that ancient road
with the camel trains,
knifing my way through hills rising
like mounds of elephants' bones
bleached white by the Ogaden sun;
and when that serpent-tongued gospeller
beaming conflagrations
from his single messianic eye
topples from blue pulpits in the burning sky
to die in embers of his own fire,
I will lay me down
anywhere that sleep surprises me,
spreading my goatskin on the opulent sand
watching low stars and the eyes of jackals
kindle like torches on ramparts of night.
Listening, with my ear pressed to the ground,
I'll hear wild flowers growing,
and the night wind,
winging its way from the Arabian Sea
as quietly as fish eagles,
will whisper secrets as old as sin to me,
resurrecting the muffled tramp of soldiers from Axum
marching to the tune of drums and flutes
and sharp commands barked by mounted Centurions;
caravans bedding down for a long night;
minstrels serenading camels in the moonlight;
concubines strumming lutes and mandolins indifferently;

sleepy camel drivers muttering obscenities
in the name of the Prophet;
masters bellowing for their slaves;
and from another age wafted sounds will
sneak into my mind's ear;
Janissaries of the Ottomans
shattering plangent silences
with the martial rhythm of cymbals,
announcing the sly traders in bazaars,
ebony farmers in sorghum fields
and golden horizons of ripening corn,
that it was tribute-time again.
I'll take the high road to Harar,
the Freedom Road,
and walk past dusty Dire Dawa in the morning
just after the rains
when the verging sand is littered with wild flowers
and the thorn trees are green.
For the Emperor's no longer there
perched on a gilded throne
with sorcerers bending his royal ear,
whispering of tiny treacheries,
while at the ornate palace gates
tall Danakil guards spring up overnight, they say,
like a spawn of Dragon's Teeth
from Fertile valleys of the Nile,
to stand as still as Cushite monuments.
These sentinels from legends of Orphir
smile imperceptibly as they hear,
clearer than Coptic bells at Eastertime,
titanic tides of mounting rage
gathering from icy Siemen peaks
to the scorching Ogden plains.
Not long ago, the Emperor,
had turned his hooded eyes away
from armies of the innocent dead
parading aimlessly across the Wollo plains
where Famine, that agate-heart robber,

stole a million lives.
While vultures, too gorged with human flesh to fly,
fell from the sky like stones,
the Emperor fed steaks
to sated lions drowsing at the palace gates;
and in the emptiness, Barons of the Land,
walked hand in hand with Death,
measuring vacant lots with greedy eyes.
How long can a man live
with a million piercing cries of pain
exploding in hollow casements of his brain
echoing tyrannies as old as crocodiles!
Mengistu felt tides of rage
rising inside his lion's heart;
but the anger of one man's son ebbs away like rivers in the Afar
sands after the rains.
The molten magma of Mengistu's wrath
Joined tributaries of fire
Flowing from thirty million hearts.
'First we must change our way of thinking', he said,
'then together we will shape hammers and anvils,
For if you're a hammer, you must strike!'
I'll take the high road to Harar again,
the Freedom Road,
crossing parched throats of dusty riverbeds,
following the camel trains;
I'll walk beside Gallah women,
Who bold as burnished moonlight,
Have long since cast aside their Moslem veils
to scan boiling horizons with fearless eyes.
I'll walk into the future with these lissome belles
Who smell of honey-wine and wild sage.
The lion-hearted Mengistu
has opened the palace gates wide
for the first time since Taharka,
the Pharoah with black velvet skin,
had ordered his High Priests
to chant orisons to deaf gods

in Temples of Isis;
or Sheba looked on Solomon with silken eyes;
or Claudius, the crippled god,
who sent ambassadors from Rome
to trade in wild beasts and rainbow-coloured slaves.
Outside ancient battlements of Harar
where caissons of the Janissaries still creak
in the night wind,
the jackals have been driven to their lairs,
they cannot stand the blinding glare,
for between the morning of awakening and victory
are thirty million incandescent hearts of fire.

I'll take the high road to Harar,
The Freedom Road,
And walk past Dira Dawa in the morning
Just after the rains,
When the verging sand is littered with wild flowers
And the thorn trees are green.

Havana, 11 February 1978

Our Home

Our Caribbean
a bandolier
of emerald isles
circling
the waist
of twin continents,
suspended
miraculously
between Atlantic deeps
and the sun;
archipelago of famished hearts
manacled
with silver sands
caged
inside
moon-burnished seas,
behind the flash
of cotton eyes
and tiger-orchid teeth
secret Fanonesque dreams
linger.
Our Caribbean
where sufferers laugh and sing
to keep from crying.

Poems of Resistance
and Liberation

For Wilson Harris

Guyana, Guyana
he knows the legends
he cares for the mysteries
he speaks like a prophet of day-clean!
he looks at
the night sky
and stars are mirrored
in his eyes
he wears his heritage
of terror and the time
like mists
at Ikowan
and Arian Island
anchors off savoy
epic heroes
inhabit his magical world
of Omai
and Palace of the Peacock
Guyana, Guyana
he knows the legends
and he cares for the mysteries

The Children

I saw the children – black, brown, yellow and white –
pacing famished pavements
their angel-eyes glittered insanely
and immortal longings shrieked
behind sirens
as the President drove by
hiding from the children's rage
behind bullet-proof shields.
Sycophants throw flowers at the President
and he smiles and waves a shaman's stick
hoping that benevolent spirits
would ensure
that he would never
go to sleep in power
and wake up in Hell.
But the wake of sirens was strewn
with ill omens of blossoms in the dust
and mingling with the children's tears.

Allende's Daughter

Living close to an Ocean Sea
I have encountered death
in many guises
and this has made me
somewhat jaded
But she was fresh
as mornings at Omai
and when she turned
and smiled at me
Easter bells echoed in my head.
All the while,
she was pining quietly
She could not
Forgive herself for not dying
Side by side
With her father, our brother-man,
Allende
She took her life
When there was still so much more
To share
With us.

Yvette

Three years later
and too soon, too soon,
the memory fades
like light in the gloaming
or conquered pain
filtering through veins of darkness
off indifferent Barbadian reefs.
And yet the death of one innocent
a single brown-skinned girl
from Guyana's heartland
and dark rivers
where caimans dream
struck home
like an arrow shaft
in the liver
when I discovered
that my nephew's wife
fresh as a morning flower
was her sister.
The assassins are still prowling
like a poisoned wind
waiting to gust in our faces
again and again
lest we forget

Barbados, 1980

Dobru Speaks to the Children

'Each generation must, out of relative obscurity discover its own mission.'
Franz Fanon

Dobru, I heard you reading for the people
giving them back their dreams
you were a cantor in green cathedrals
where Njukas and Saramacas
turned a raging river
into sanctuaries for them
and graves for enemies
you were a ju-ju priest
with fire on your tongue
Nyankapon, the sky-god
spoke through you
and scattered borrowed dreams
the whiter than snow dreams
the blonde hair dreams
the bluest eye dreams
and drowned them
as Wonotoba does
in whirlpools of dark water.
Dobru, I saw the children listening
the wide enchantment in their eyes
mirrored your poems
each word became a speck of blood
a drop of spring water
Dobru, that night
I thought I saw the children listening again
asleep, dreaming
and talking in their sleep they said
they heard
footfalls of a tiger
creeks with serpent tongues
Wonotoba's fury after the rains

the silent rage of Amazonian trees
and ancestors
with voices soft as the flow of sap
in tall trees
I heard
the listening children sigh
and waking realized that
you'd given them back lost dreams.

Assassins of Dreams

They'll try to kill me
rub me out
erase my name
from the register of the living
as soon as they discover
how my dreams
span distances
wider than galaxies
or my love
for the wretched
is fathomless.
Through a spectrum of their lust
for Empires
upon which the sun never sets
or for the sun's sweat, gold,
they'll never see me as I am
a tall brown man
wearing macaws for epaulettes
and starlight for a crown.
Assassins will be lurking
in the eaves
like black mambas
ready to strike,
sensors in their forked tongues
will detect
hot passions kindling
in the furnace-core
of my soul.
They'll try to kill me
rub me out, erase my name
from the register of the living
as soon as they discover
how my dreams
span distances
wider than galaxies

or my love for the wretched
is fathomless.
But I'll defy the dreamkillers,
tantalize them with poem-hymns,
mock them with immortal vibes
hidden in verses.
Dreamkillers can never erase
a charango
strumming melodies
or panpipes fluting lyrics
from a songless lyre.

Evanston, 17 May 1979

Canadian Poems

Snowtime

Last night
moonlight veined fields of snow
with shadows
naked trees
gazed at their images
and sighing
swayed from side to side
like dancers
with imprisoned feet

The Cyclopean Eye

My foreday morning dream lingers
like dew in chalices of balsa flowers,
and on cool evenings tinamous sing;
bees click their feet like castanets.
Tomorrow and tomorrow
hoarse cocks,
heralds of death
rehearse their fabled calls all night;
death skulks in tall savannah grass;
streets of eternity rush past
twisted sentinels of saman trees.
But in my exile North
earth wears glaciers,
bandaging a wrinkled brow;
Antaeus is frozen in palaces of ice
between earth and a cruel sky,
and one eyed Cyclops peers through borealis light
at distant suns.

The Exile

Exile trumpets
come north to Labrador, Baffin
Greenland of the snowbirds!
Borealis twilights shatter
in a spray of curlews
south to the bitter corn
and the sun,
circling
totems of eyeless sunflowers
and hibiscus
with pistils
like parched tongues.
I answer the call
North
of Hatteras
homing
to harsh seasons.
Frobisher came
to part the ice
startling snowbirds
white against white
sundering the dream of
Polar Bears
Winter sun explodes,
icy sparks
that prick my heart
like tattoos on my skin.
Longboats
ply tides of my grief.
Evenings, dark as my skin
overflow the sky's rim
like a limping tide
of blood and smashed brains.
I am chained to my rock
facing north;

Prometheus,
blinded by vultures
and raging when he lost his sight
felt the same pang
in his flesh.
I would have fled to stars
a stowaway
with cosmonauts
and spent millenniums
whirling with asteroids, galaxies,
comets, suns, constellations,
seven brooding moons of Venus.
I am Antaeus in reverse
severing
my blood-knot with
earths that mothered me
I wander in voids at nights
I immolate myself
rising out of ashes
white as my eyes
in the mornings…
death's swifter than light.
South
where curlews escape.
Blow, blow,
the sun's no less unkind
than winter winds.
Blossoms of bougainvillea,
poinsettias, croton, wild azaleas,
daisies and sweet simitu….
bluebells
sleeping through the night
in gardens of Ichillibar,
commit unspeakable cruelties
poisoning hummingbirds,
binding the tongues of
nightingales, blue sackees and trumpeter birds
Curlews

Hurtling through the sun
like arrowheads
send shadows
scampering
past Everglades, the Bayous,
green islands and jade seas.
Trade winds
harpooning stars
with flying fish
mark trails with spume
and the long sea swells
curlews embrace
long savannahs
and the green rains.
But curlews return in the Spring,
screaming
for leaves soft as foam.

Morning at Lake Simcoe

A seagull dead, dead,
hung white as bones
on a tree in autumn;
with wings spread out like petals
and the beak , a pistil
stained with red.
I followed the spoor of the bird's pain
stumbled on hunters
raping the day.
they shot the sun on the wing
wild hunters with guns,
blind as rocks;
the wind sent white horses
to pluck the morning out of the lake
before it drowned.
pines enfiladed the wounded sun
until it broke away from moorings
in the green lake
a fireball
wheeling across the east wind
and the mists
elms and beaches blushed
bright as satellite suns
before the east wind
stripped them naked
and petted them with cold fingers
and lecherous lips.
virgin trees
pressed against the clamour of the wind
hypnotized by the insistent
and melodious whisperings
'We're offering sweet sap
from the roots of our lives!' they cried
The wind was their undoing….
and mine.

morning emptied its trough of dreams
into the green lake;
the palsied sun grew strong
Fluted sunbeams clashed
with the raucous singing of crows;
the sleeping rocks awoke
and stirred like seals.

A seagull, dead, dead
falling leaves spin away,
leaves, golden or red as sleepless eyes,
erasing the footprints of hunters
on a razzia with guns
on the trail of orgasms
laughing as they scattered the hours
like feathers with blood-stains.
A careless hunter shot
one seagull and the sun.
The sun is certain of its resurrection.

The Hemlock Fringe Before the Pines

The hemlock fringe before the pines
speaking in the wind
and dancing like a ballerina
with imprisoned feet
I'm not as lonely as I might have been
when hemlocks sway
and sunsets sing
sweet chariots low

25 December 1994

Morning Writes a Calligraphy with Shadows

Morning writes a calligraphy with shadows
on the Spring snows
the first day of Spring
leaning out of a cradle
and the bearded trees
baby-sitting.
Let steep escarpments of my lingering pain
bewitch new seasons,
fling the wind like a lariat: and listen
is that an infant crying
or the wind?
Ambushed and released by seasons of adventure I came
and found the nights
strewn with wild flowers
when she breathed beside me
her flesh was wild azaleas
her breath jasmine,
her touch daffodils
her lips hibiscus
her body bending like canna lilies
and lotus scattered for Dupa Vali
she was the fragrant earth
and wild daisies of my awakening.

Star Poems

Canis Major

Canis, the neighbour of Puppis and Lepus
and Sirius
the Hound of Heaven
guarding galaxies.

Canis Minor

Canis, reaping stars
and gathering the harvest
south
near Hydra and Monoceros
where Procyon, the lapdog
wears the brightest jewel of all.

Canopus One

Canopus on the Nile
and the temple to Serapis
where young initiates
dark and lithe as reeds
serve wine
to priests murmuring
orisons
to the indifferent tides.
Royal messengers from Alexandria arrive
panting to announce the pharaoh!
The priests scatter like birds
to recite incantations of welcome
with a monotonous zeal
under the eye of High Priestesses
of Isis.

Canopus Two

The eye of god in Paradise
Six hundred and fifty light years
from planet earth:
the second brightest star
in the constellation Carina.

Nostalgia

Dreamtime

The dreamtime came with morning's awakening
when butterflies jewelled landscapes
with no shape, no meaning, no life;
The dreamtime brought
star infested heliconias
morphos with sleepless eyes
on incandescent wings
somber caligos with monkish cowls and capes
and monarchs strewn like fallen stars.
Pia and Makunaima,
heroes of the dreamtime
brought fire,
freed wind from prisons in the firmament,
flung rivers like shining lariats
from secret springs.
That's why the living world wears green,
rivers sing requiems to drown
a boatman's dream,
mountains impale the moon on icy nights,
the cruel sun-wheel spins in daytime,
night stars cool burning faces.
That's why I'm here
sunning myself in the dreamtime,
writing you a poem.

Manaharva's Dream

A cloud of azure Morpho butterflies
crossed Potaro at sunrise and imprinted shadows
on a timeless mirror of still water.
One butterfly lingered
and dangled like a jewelled pendant
on the breast of the morning.
Flamingoes, red as flame flowers,
hung like lanterns
from the bearded trees
at sunset.
Night came and claimed
its swift suzerainty of darkness
And mesmerized by the songless singing of Ewe drums
I worshipped Carib gods
under a shower of stars.
My altars were carpeted with fallen leaves
and a piper owl fluted haunting melodies .
Foreday morning winds and sunlight swept aside
billowing opaque morning mists.
Hummingbirds awakening from a dreamless sleep
embroidered rainbows onto the unsullied fabric of air
before they danced and darted to plunder pollen from heliconias.
A sleek kingfisher shattered mirror images
of blue skies and sentinel trees.
Potaro stirred and joined the running tides
that rushed to
vent their insane rage
of white water
at Tumatumari.

27 August 2004

South, to the Land

South, to the land
where the curlews go!
The brutal South –
blossoms of bougainvillea in the dust,
blood and beauty.
Bluebells, sleeping through the fragrant night
in gardens like the Shalimar
commit unspeakable cruelties
in the day light poisoning
innocent hummingbirds,
binding the tongues of larks and kiskadees.
Then singing birds no longer trill
the piercing melodies of my awakening.
South, where the curlews fly!
Past the everglades, and the blue-green seas,
and islands, a necklace of emeralds and jade,
caught in a bellows of sea and sky,
vomiting Trade Winds.
Flying fish, leaping like a memory of stars!
Curlews, parting the windstreams, tunneling
South, always South
to long savannahs and the warm rains.

But curlews return in the spring,
screaming their delight
at life quickening:
Leaves soft as foam,
the innocent grass,
and March winds, brushing sleep
from the bear's eyes.
Summer brings back the sun's fever
and I die!

Daydreaming

Tomorrow ...
        always tomorrow

Put offs and put ons

Existing in a life
        as incomplete
        as this poem

Joanna

Joanna's passing
was a chronicle of pain.
The big C stole her life,
snuffed out her laughter
and left a legacy of tears
for three generations
of women in the family.
The howling silences
the agony,
was something
that no one could really share
with the victims.
Dying, Joanna remembered
the good times
and the salad days.
I am glad I was not there
to see her become
a shadow of herself
I remember her as she was
in days gone by
with burnished
copper-coloured hair
and blue-green eyes
occasionally touched with grey
and kindling
from ashes of her discontent
to fire.

The Survivor

She felt it
like reaper's scythe
in the marrow, limping
She cursed God
and vilified His name
The Beautiful Ones
carrying Bibles
like divine insurance policies
on Sundays
hurried by
murmuring
'it would indeed be merciful
if the demented beggar
died'
Twenty and five years later
with pain
like daggers in her brain
she was alive
cursing God
and laughing at the skies
In the meantime
Mantop, Death's messenger-boy,
had snatched
the Beautiful Ones away
even though
they'd never known an ache
in their lives.

Love Poems

Eternity

Eternity, she whispered
and her eyes
bright as obsidian knives
made four with mine.

Eternity?
A fortnight passed,
and when my love came back to me
cosmic ecstasies subside
under a trysting tree.

Chantoba

Chantoba of the rented gardens
discovering herself in the new moon's season of love
lilies and mimosas
and forget-me-nots loitering
in shadows of wild azaleas
the smell of her flesh lingers like incense even now
when ages have gone by
I wait to hear a single wild murmur of escape
but she is caged, gilded banalities of youth and age
chain her
I would have torn asunder
ramparts of heaven for Chantoba
Yesterday

Chantoba II

Morning writes shadowed pictographs
on late Spring snows.
Bewitched again
by promises of new seasons
I remember, I remember
seasons of adventure
strewn with wildest flowers
and, Chantoba, beside me
her flesh, wild azaleas
her touch, a gentle morning wind
leaning on daffodils;
her body lissome, long-stemmed
like canna lilies;
herself, fragrant earth
under mute snows
waiting
for a daisy's awakening.

April Twentieth

Shantoba arrived
facing the sunshine
on a Spring morning
She glittered like a seal
slipping out of amniotic ease
and her first cry
sounded like a sea-chanty
Her eyes
dark as quiescent seas
off *Gracias a Dios*
were thoughtful.
The first time I held her
I felt my heart leap
high as galaxies.
Greeting the Spring morning
with a wild cry,
glistening like a seal
she swam
out of her amniotic ease
into our tumultuous lives.
Her first cry
sounded like a sea-song to me.

Evanston, 20 April 1982

For Joy

The meadowlarks
that sing
in spring
can send my heart
awandering
The silences
of wintertime
when I drowse
at a fireside
fill me with longings
for meadowlarks
to sing again.

Louisville, 24 November 2004

To Joy

Even now
I love big brown eyes that caress like silk
ever and ever sad and laughing eyes
whose lids make such sweet shadows when they close
it seems another beautiful look of hers
I love her fresh mouth
ahh her scented mouth
and curving hair
subtle as smoke
and light fingers
and laughter of green gems

Cicada Song

Cicadas fluted so melodiously
that I remembered her
moonbeams ribbed the sea
and the wind
with a muted rage
forced the trees
to bend their heads low
lambs bleated and a baby cried
the sky was wide
a garner holding land and sea
and yet it could not hold
the memory of her
the sweet untrammeled memory
of hours locked in your embrace
bursting like galaxies inside my head
I need her as my flesh needs sun
Cicadas sang low rhapsodies
and palm trees stirred
the way my heart does
thinking of her –
my girl
Cicadas sang a love song for my girl
and I walked on a starlit beach
past sacred groves
where Hindus burn the dead
on sandalwood pyres
my girl alone with me
side by side
the golden sand
warm underneath our feet
Cicadas sang a lovesong from my girl
I'm sending her
this wild cicada song

Africa

Ballad for Soweto

Mandela, Mandela,
young simbas in the pride
have been sleeping like lemurs
with eyes wide open.
Listening, they heard white rogue-elephants
trampling down the innocent grass;
small veld fires spreading into conflagrations;
cicadas fluting warnings
outside the ravaged kraals:
and drunks in the shabeens
shouting mad orisons to freedom
in the late and limpid moonlight.
Mandela, Mandela,
young simbas in the pride
heard elders sighing in their sleep;
the simpering wind eroding granite patience,
until soft sibilant breathing
erupted into murmurings
of rebellion.
Mandela, Mandela,
young simbas in the pride
with their ears pressed to barren mountainsides
heard your hoarse voice thundering
across the veld's silence,
and saw jackals scattering.
They heard you pacing, pacing
like a black leopard
up and down the cold floors
of your demented Robben Island cell;
and your heart beating, beating
like Bemba drums.

Gems and Dust

A single cry,
sharper than accouri thorns
pierced eardrums
of midnight miners
tunneling to claim Klerksdorp's gold.
Mpolo was buried alive
in a rockfall
and his terminal scream
keeps echoing.
One mile above
the innocent elephant grass
sings a requiem to him.
North of the Limpopo,
under the sun's insane eye,
Mpolo's wife and children, five,
waited for news
deep inside the Rift valley's silence.
When the letter arrived
(he couldn't write
and she couldn't read),
Jumo, the village scribe
squatted amidst
a cluster of listeners and huts
hunched like sleeping buffalos,
and read unctuously,
while Leza, Mpolo's wife,
carried her fear
closer than sweat to a pore
inside her.
'Dear woman of my life,
I asked, as usual, my friend Ezekiel
to write this letter,
for white leaves
that speak
to the listening ear

and the inquisitive eye
remain a mystery to me.
My own sweet woman,
your Mpolo loves you
like a kudu loves fresh green grass
after the rains;
and all the raindrops in the sky
or all the sands of the Kalahari
can't tally my love for you.
I'll come home
before the next small moon
starts ripening.'
The mines at Klerksdorp
filled Mpolo's mouth
and the sockets of his eyes
with gems and dust,
but his heart
still beats easily
inside a granite mountain
and his spirit
singing in elephant grass
lives.

For Dennis Brutus

He lashed them
with the lariat tip
of his poet's pen;
his words stabbed
like awaraballi pimplas
deep inside
their cruel brains
puncturing their ballooned pride,
deflating their herenvolk myth.
He was our troubadour
singing defiance
across oceans and continents
lashing them with words
that struck like lightning.
they tried to silence him
with a bullet in the back
in Jo'burg, but
he rose again
singing freedom.
In the old days
he had the malice
to be
a poet and a long distance runner.
Running against the sun
his limbs devoured
marathon and cross country distances.
They sent him
to Robben Island's granite fisted hell,
and manacled,
he shared rock-breaking
with Sisulu, the lion hearted
with Mandela, the bravest of the brave.
He penned his *Letters to Martha*
in the fogbound Hades
affirming

that poetry
was like lightning
and lightning
can never be timid.

The History-Maker

Walter, Walter
I can still hear your voice
soft as silk
intoning like a seer's
on my front porch
while Georgetown
squatted around us
on a careless afternoon
and a hungry urchin's eyes
gauged the time
when Mr. Bourne's mangoes
would reach a golden ripening.
You, the fearless Bonita,
my old mother and I
noticed in a thrice
the dark child's searching.
My mother, shading inward looking and oracular eyes
that knew so well
the vertigo-glare of Guyana's sun
for ninety years,
discerned for an instant
a stealthy and insane secret.
Her ancient eyes made four
with your young ones,
you smiled,
assuaging her concern,
and retreated behind a curtain of pleasantries
while hungry dogs barked in alleyways
and girls from the 'Sisters of Mercy College'
fluttered past like heliconia butterflies.

Walter, Walter,
you and my old mother knew
that you would die like a comet
illuminating dark firmaments for dreamers,

galaxies for survivors of the cruelest crossing,
from Africa, India, the lean and hungry Azores
the barrios of China, and Europe's mean fringes.
We had lost faith
until you returned
and spoke the words
and lived the deeds
You made it clear as water in a spring
that Black is mystery, Black is strength,
Black is the colour of Sudanic longings
Dogon dreams of Sirius, the Hound of Heaven,
spawned on Turkana's shores when dawns were young
and homo sapiens
was staggering away from a cradle
between the blue Nile and the white,
the lakes with verging reeds
and the clamorings of a billion birds.
These siblings of our earliest beginnings
invested planet earth with the first Black dreams,
Black love, Black singing,
Black poem-hymns to the dead and the living
until wanderlust
sent ancestors of the dreamtime roaming.
and the sun in their blood spoke too softly
for listening ears to hear.

Walter, Walter,
you were a roots-man,
grounding with the brothers
during moon bursts
deep inside gullies
of the Rasta Man's suffering,
a scholar-man, a renaissance Guyana-man.
You walked with the scorned,
the despised cast-asides,
the rejected,
the ones outside everything
the plundered ones

limeing on the Streets of Eternity
with leftover time to kill.
They opened surly casements
of their wounded hearts
and let you in,
And listening to a litany of hurts
you inspired them.
into taking their place in the tournament
against Imperialism
where the stakes for which they jousted
were liberty or a long oblivion.

Walter, Walter,
dying, you taught us that a man
was more than his shadow
and as much as his ultimate sacrifice.
This is no requiem
it's a banner furling higher than Roraima
for you and I have always known
that only the poor in spirit really die.
Your spirit of air, water, and fire is alive
murder has failed to bind the enchantment of your tongue.

Epilogue

Your words keep echoing inside our heads
Like a bellbird's song.
It is as though having awakened sleeping hearts
you left orchestras of talking drums to sound alarms
lest we should lapse
into a dreaming torpor of slowtime again.
Parting, the last time you met,
Your mother said,
'Take care, walk well.' And then
news of your searing death wounded her like an assegai
and keening like an amarata in the wind
she sang aloud her lamentation

'Dear Jesus, have mercy on his young soul,
and may his murderers
taste ashes and aloes in their throats
until they choke
with putrid earth and the smoke from hell-fires
Jesus, my redeemer,
give me strength to bear this mother's grief,
two fruits of my womb were smeared with clots of blood
at birth and in the midst of dying.
I curse again those carrion-men
who pushed this chosen son
into an exit of death.
Guyana, beware!
The living dead are prowling everywhere
skulking across our violated land,
scavenging for lives;
this is a time of jackals
carrion crows, High Priests of the burial ground,
we must arise and fight
or turning our backs to the sun,
bend low like slaves
and kiss our shadows,
Weep not for my proud son, let us instead
shout defiance
across these final seasons of my waning years,
For if they stole his life in the evening time,
they'll come with the rising sun for ours.'

Walter, Walter, you slept to dream through childhood,
lying down wherever weariness surprised you
but when you became a man
you woke up to discover that when you dream alone
it's only a dream,
but when you dream with millions,
the dream's like a flower awakening
to trumpet new dawns of reality.
Your enemies and mine
still lurk inside abysmal chasms of their fear

serving the vampires in disguise
who occupy Guyana's Halls of Shame,
her labyrinthine corridors of power.
Go in peace and love, walk well.
For one morning
while you're listening to the sound of roots
marrying the dark earth,
and sap flowing in stems of wild flowers
you'll hear all of a sudden
the thunder of famished hearts you touched,
chorusing your words
inheriting the victory that you preached
with your tongue of fire
and beheld with your eyes of dawn
and afterwards
as long as the grass grows
and leaves clap hands applauding in the wind
we'll carry your memory like pennants of flame
deep inside the incandescent sun.

Geneva, 17 June 1980

For Irving Davis

He won his race
with the African sun
knowing
that night
pulped memories
of ancient hurts
between
Black hands.
He relived
Sargasso crossings
of ancestral slaves
carrying back
his trans-Atlantic dream
of Black Freedom
in the holds
of aeroplanes
like Malcolm
had done
until they both
touched down
on their African earth
their African homeland.
He was never
a stranger
anywhere
that he could declare
the shining essences
of his dream.
They tried
to snuff out
his dream
in Dar-es-Salaam
but only succeeded
in crippling
a leg.

Afterwards
he limped his way
to the vanguard again
and stayed there.
His dream
was a magic salve
against strewn hurts
waiting to ambush him.
He was a dream-merchant
selling merchandise
from factories
of Black liberation.
He died with the certainty that production was increasing
and new markets
secreted in hearts of millions
were opening every year.

Dahomey Dreams

Boukman, Macandal,
the canecutters are restless again
their machetes flash
earthing the lightning
of revolution,
Legba,
Squats under a silk cotton tree
patient as a mountain
his silence is all encompassing
but when he growls
and stands up straight,
hills bleached to the bone
will wear green again
Dahomey drums
will speak again
Cocks of day-clean
will crow again
Toussaint
will thunder
across slopes
of Cap Haitien again
Dessalines,
Vigilant as ever,
will trample
his crown
in mud
And ride
With cavalries
Of liberty again.
Christophe
will bequeath
his royal accoutrements
to a museum
in the Citadel
and ride

with parrots
for epaulettes
and eagle feathers
for a crown
spirits of the Lightning – Eel
the Thunder-Axe
will sing again:
'Caonabo, Caonabo,
Our first Freedom Fighter,
Are tides of Sargasso
Still plucking your bones
With a murmur of panpipes?
Does Ojeda's betrayal
still burn
in your throat
like hot embers
at mosquito-time?
Caonabo, Caonabo,
leave your ocean-tomb
of sea fans, chitons
and cold anemones,
wake up Ancestor Caonabo, Wake up!
Fidel and Neto
have healed
your wounded dream.'

Epitaph

A Quiet Passing

I feel at 50 prepared to meet death
And yet to tell you the truth
I'm not really ready to die
I'm evading the thought of it in my mind
and allowing it to slip away
like a snake in tall grass
that shivers in the wind
Sometimes I dream of dying gloriously
Banners flaring
and guns bringing me down
and then I'd lie in the dust with
flies licking the lips of my wounds.
But, other times I dream of dying quietly
slipping away
like a falling tide does out to sea
I'm even afraid to write about dying,
Mantop, might be loitering
in the shadows
But it's not dying that's important
it's living, and the quality of life
Sometimes I'd like them to build
monuments to me
and then again
I'd rather not
Just let me lie
Close to some green shore
where Potaro sings requiems
to entomb bones and gems
and a boatman's dreams.
Let me lie quietly
listening to wild azaleas grow
quietly quietly quietly.

Notes

The Nomad
A.J. Seymour (1914-1989) was a Guyanese poet, essayist and editor of the journal *Kyk-Over-Al*.

Africa – America
Kwame Nkrumah (1909-1972) led Ghana to independence and was its first President (1957-1966). He was overthrown in a coup in 1966.

Aiomon Kondi
Aiomon Kondi is the god of creation in Arawakian Indian mythology.

Florida – Angola
Osceola was a Seminole (Indian) leader who successfully fought against the US military in Georgia and Florida during a key period of the 30-year Seminole wars. This protracted guerilla action lasted from 1820s to 1850s. The Seminole Indians were a mixture of indigenous people and escaped African slaves. Osceola was eventually tricked and captured and died in captivity.

Florida – Angola II
Kofi Abraham and Atlassa were Seminole Indians who picked up the fallen standard of Osceola in the Seminole Wars.

Caonabo
Caonabo was an Amerindian Cacique (chief) in Hispaniola when Columbus landed in 1492. In an attempt to repulse the Spanish colonial presence, Caonabo and his soldiers destroyed the Fort Natividad settlement.

Alonzo de Ojeda (1468-1515) was a Spanish conquistador who travelled to Hispaniola on Columbus' second voyage in 1493. He became the first Governor of the new colony and tricked Caonabo into thinking that they would be negotiating a peace. He captured Caonabo and sent the Cacique to Spain as a souvenir for the King. Caonabo died en route.

The Cliffs at Manzanilla
Roberto Retamar (1930-) is a Cuban poet and essayist.

A Chrysalis of Rainbows
Julien Fedon (1749-1796) was one of the free Black freedom fighters in eighteenth-century Grenada; he led the 1795 Fedon rebellion. Augusto Cesar Sandino (1895-1934) was a revolutionary leader in Nicaragua who led a six-year guerilla fight against US troops in an attempt to prevent the spread of US control of agricultural, mining and other interests in the country. Sandino was an inspiration to the 1979 revolutionaries who called themselves the Sandinistas.

Toussaint L'Ouverture
Toussaint L'Ouverture (1743-1803) was a Haitian hero who, in 1791, led the first and only successful slave rebellion in the Caribbean. He was later captured by the French and died in captivity in France in 1803.

Jean Jacques Dessalines (1758-1806) was a former slave and first Leader of the Republic of Haiti, 1804-1806. He took the title of Emperor after that of Napoleon. He was assassinated. Henry Christophe (1767-1820) was King of Haiti from 1811-1818.

Obote Must Return
Apollo Milton Obote (1925-2005) led Uganda to its independence in 1962 and was its first President. He was overthrown by Idi Amin in 1971.

Who Pays the Piper?
In 1961, a CIA sponsored invasion of Cuba, known as the Bay of Pigs invasion, was defeated after three days by the Cuban armed forces under the command of Fidel Castro.

Ballad for a Revolution
Kaierouanne was an Amerindian leader in Grenada in the mid-seventeenth century who fought against the invading Europeans.

Tribute to Dobru
Robin Ravales Dobru (1935-1983) was a poet and writer from Surinam.

For Buzz
Edward Palmer (Buzz) is a Chicago-based African American activist and co-founder of The People Programme.

Lost Steps I Found, II
Alejo Carpentier (1904-1980) was a Cuban novelist; *The Lost Steps* is his most famous novel.

Tribute to Claudia
Claudia Jones (1915-1964) was a Trinidad-born journalist. She was imprisoned in the US for her involvement in the Communist Party and deported in 1955 to the UK. In London she founded Britain's first Black newspaper, *The West Indian Gazette*, and helped establish the first Notting Hill Carnival in 1959. She is buried in Highgate Cemetery next to Karl Marx.

Requiem for Ted Watkins
Ted Watkins was an African American professional football player who played a prominent role in the Black Power movement in Toronto, Canada. He was shot by a white liquor store owner while visiting his wife and son in California, US.

Requiem for Andrew
Andrew Salkey (1928-1995) was a Jamaican poet and writer. *Come Home, Malcolm Heartland* was one of his novels. Paul Bogle (1820-1865) was a Baptist minister and revolutionary hero in Jamaica. Jose Marti (1853-1853) was a writer and revolutionary. He is a national hero of Cuba. Marcus Garvey (1887-1940) was a Jamaican activist who became the leader of a major black nationalist movement in the US in the early 1900s. His Universal Negro Improvement Association was an inspiration to Blacks not only in the US, but around the world in the post-War War I period.

Rather than surrender, he and his followers chose to throw themselves off a cliff. Maurice Bishop (1943-1983) led the New Jewel Movement in Grenada and overthrew President Gairy in 1979. He became President, but was killed in a coup in 1983. Anacoana was the Cacique Caonabo's wife on the island of Hispaniola at the time of Columbus' early voyages. She became the Cacique after his death in 1493.

Grenada! Grenada!
In 1983 the US invaded Grenada following an internal power-struggle in the leadership of the New Jewel Movement.

I Fight for What Must Be
The Sharpeville massacre occurred in 1960 in South Africa when thousands of Black residents rose up in protest of the pass laws of the Apartheid regime. Sixty-nine people were killed and 150 injured.

If He's Killed We'll Bleed
Mumia Abu-Jamal (1954-) is a political activist. Sentenced to death in 1982 for shooting a police officer, he has become the subject of a series of mass campaigns for his release. Over these 33 years, he has also become a prolific writer. Malcolm X (1925-1965) was a Black Muslim leader in the US. He was assassinated in New York in 1966.

Letter to Agostinho Neto
Agostinho Neto (1922-1979) was a poet and the revolutionary leader of Angola. He was also the country's first President, 1975-1979.

The Death of Lumumba
Patrice Lumumba (1925-1961) helped lead his country to independence; in 1960 he was the first Prime Minister of the Democratic Republic of the Congo. He was assassinated in 1961. Maurice Mpolo, Minister of Youth in the Lumumba administration, and Joseph Okito, former Vice-President of the Senate, were killed alongside Lumumba.

Requiem for Cheddi Jagan
Cheddi Jagan (1918-1997) was Premier of British Guiana from 1961 to 1964 and President of Guyana from 1992 to 1997.

On Visiting Philip Agee
Phillip Agee (1935-2008) was a former CIA agent who turned against the agency, exposing many of its secrets. He lived the rest of his life in exile in Germany.

Requiem For Warren
Warren Thorpe (d. 1996) was a highly-regarded Barbadian educator and Jan Carew's brother in-law.

Requiem for Vernon
Vernon Jarrett (1918-2004) was an award-winning African American journalist in Chicago.

For Martin Carter
Martin Carter (1927-1997) was a Guyanese poet and political activist, who was twice imprisoned by colonial British authorities for his involvement in the struggle for Guyanese independence.

Ten Years: 1959-1969
Camilo Cienfuegos Gorriaran (1932-1959) was a major figure in the Cuban revolution. Simon Bolivar (1783-1830) was a Venezuelan freedom fighter whose efforts to liberate northern and western South America from Spain led to the establishment of Gran Colombia in 1821. The country Bolivia is named after him. Nat Turner (1800-1831), a former slave, led a famous slave rebellion in Virginia in 1831. John Brown (1800-1859) was a white abolitionist who led the infamous raid on Harper's Ferry in 1859. Owen Brown, John Anthony Copeland, jr, John Kaggi and Shields Green (Emperor Green) were also involved in the raid.

For Wilson Harris
Wilson Harris (1921-) is a Guyanese writer and Jan Carew's brother in-law. *Palace of the Peacock* is one of his novels.

Allende's Daughter
Salvador Allende (1908-1973) was the President of Chile from 1971 to 1973. He died during the US-backed Pinochet coup. Beatriz Allende was the daughter of Salvador Allende. Married to a Cuban diplomat posted to Santiago, she went into exile in Cuba following the coup. She later took her own life.

Dobru Speaks to the Children
Franz Fanon (1925-1961) was Martiniquan revolutionary and philosopher.

Canis Majoris
The great dog is a southern constellation between Puppis and Orion containing Sirius the dog star; the brightest star.

Canis Minor
The little or lesser dog is a small southern constellation west of Orion and south of Gemini containing the bright star Procyon (lesser dog).

Canopus One
Canopus One is a first magnitude star in the constellation Careria and the second brightest star in the heavens . Also an ancient sea-coast city on the eastern outskirts of modern-day Alexandria.

Chantoba
This is a love poem to Jan Carew's wife, Joy, using the name of the Guyanese Amerindian queen of the early colonial period who was known to have tricked the English colonial governor into signing a treaty with her.

April Twentieth
This poem is about the birth of Jan Carew's second daughter, named Shantoba after the Guyanese Amerindian queen of the early colonial period. The name was purposefully altered to ensure a pronunciation close to the original.

For Dennis Brutus
Dennis Brutus (1924- 2009) was a South African poet and anti-Apartheid activist.

The History Maker
Walter Rodney (1942-1980) was a Guyanese historian and activist. He was assassinated in Guyana in 1980.

For Irving Davis
Irving Davis was an African-American who worked with the National Council of Churches' programmes in the Caribbean and Africa.

Dahomey Dreams
Francois Macandal (d. 1758) was a Haitian Maroon who was born in Senegal. He was also known to draw on his voudou skills when he led a slave revolt. He was captured and publically executed. Dutty Boukman (d. 1791) was a Jamaican-born Haitian slave who took inspiration from Macandal when he led a slave revolt. He was also captured and publically executed.

Acknowledgements

Several of these poems were first published in *Streets of Eternity* (self-published, Georgetown, 1952) and *Sea Drums in My Blood* (New Voices, Trinidad, 1981).

Thanks are due to the editors of the following publications where some of these poems first appeared: *Antillian Lunen, Bim, Bite In, Black American Literature Forum, Breaklight, Caliban, Caribbean Contact, Caribbean Quarterly, De Zee de Zee: Gedichtenuit he helewereld, Journal of African Civilizations, Journal of Black Poetry, Karibsky Majak, La Revista, Like It Is, New World, New Writing in the Caribbean, Nimrod, Pacific Quarterly, Schwarzer Orpheus, The Free West Indian, The Heinemann Book of Caribbean Poetry, The Penguin Book of Caribbean Verse in English.*